HERITAGE
LANGUAGES

HERITAGE LANGUAGES

The development and denial of
Canada's linguistic resources

Jim Cummins
Marcel Danesi

Canadian Cataloguing in Publication Data

Cummins, Jim, 1949-
  Heritage languages: the development and denial
of Canada's linguistic resources

(Our schools/our selves monograph series; 5)
ISBN 0-921908-05-9 (Our Schools/Our Selves)
ISBN 0-920059-69-4 (Garamond)

1. Native language and education - Canada.
2. Linguistic minorities - Education - Canada.
3. Language Policy - Canada. I. Danesi, Marcel,
1946-   . II. Our Schools/Our Selves Education
Foundation. III. Title. IV. Series.

LC3734.C85 1990   371.97'00971   C90-093609-6

This book is published jointly by Our Schools/Our Selves Education Foundation, 1698 Gerrard Street East, Toronto, Ontario, M4L 2B2 and Garamond Press, 67A Portland Street, Toronto, Ontario, M5V 2M9.

For subscribers to **Our Schools/Our Selves: a magazine for Canadian education activists,** this is issue #10, the second issue of volume 2.

The subscription series **Our Schools/Our Selves** (ISSN 0840-7339) is published 8 times a year. Second class mail registration number 8010. Mailed at Centre Ville, Montréal, Québec.

Design, typesetting and art work: Goodness Graphics.

Our Schools/Our Selves production: Heather Alden, Howie Chodos, David Clandfield, Doug Little, Stephanie MacIntosh, George Martell, Liisa Repo Martell, Richard Peachey, Satu Repo, Deborah Wise Harris.

Printed in Canada by La maîtresse d'école inc., Montréal, Québec.

ACKNOWLEDGEMENTS

Preparation of this volume was supported by a grant to the Ontario Institute for Studies in Education by the Multiculturalism Directorate of the Secretary of State. We have also received financial assistance for publication from The Chinese Lingual-Cultural Centre of Canada and The Canadian Centre for Italian Culture and Education. We gratefully acknowledge this support.

We would also like to thank George Martell and David Clandfield for their helpful comments on earlier drafts of the manuscript and for their support in completing the volume. A number of people provided important feedback on the fifth chapter dealing with bilingualism among the Deaf community. We would particularly like to acknowledge our debt to Carolyn Ewoldt, Neita Israelite, Gary Malkowski, and Patricia Shores-Herman.

Finally, many teachers, both of heritage languages and other subjects, have inspired us by their practice and insights. In particular, we would like to thank Meilian Lam and Maria Lopes for demonstrating in their classrooms just how enriching active learning in a heritage language can be.

Table of Contents

Chapter 1

Introduction
A War of Words

Throughout human history the ability to speak several languages has always been regarded as a mark of culture and intelligence. In the past, elite groups have ensured that their children would acquire competence in two or more languages, and in most countries this is still the case. During the past 20 years in Canada, for example, middle-class professional parents have increasingly demanded that schools provide French immersion programs for their children, such that there are currently about 250,000 children in various types of French immersion program. In recent years private schools in British Columbia have offered formerly exotic languages such as Japanese to their elementary school students while the Toronto French school continues to pioneer the teaching of languages in Canada by offering instruction in Russian and German in addition to French. In general, it is common for middle-class North Americans to admire the multilingual skills of students in many European countries and to wish that they too could speak several languages with similar ease.

If multilingualism is regarded as a valuable asset both for the individual and for the society, then why do so many Canadians vehemently oppose the teaching of heritage languages?[1] Why do many parents who demand that their children be given the opportunity to become bilingual in French and English protest angrily at the fact that their tax dollars are being used to teach the languages of immigrant children? Why is it appropriate to promote multilingualism in private schools such as the Toronto French School but not in the public school system? Is multilingualism good for the rich but bad for the poor?

The extent to which provision should be made for the teaching of heritage languages has been debated at federal, provincial and local school board levels since the mid-seventies. The most volatile debates have taken place in Metropolitan Toronto where the issue has burst into public controversy on a regular basis during the past 15 years. Although the specific issues that have sparked these debates in Toronto have varied, the underlying positions and assumptions have remained largely the same. At issue are very different perspectives on the nature of Canadian society and how it should respond to population changes that are radically increasing the extent of linguistic and cultural diversity across the country. Does diversity represent a threat to Canadian unity or, should we "celebrate our differences," as urged by the slogan of a previous federal government?

Canadians are not alone in their concern about diversity. In most countries, issues surrounding ethnicity, culture and language invariably rouse the bulk of the population from their mental hibernation. The following description of perhaps the most volatile phase of the Toronto debate could equally be applied to debates about minority languages in Europe and the United States:

> In essence it [the debate] seems to be a battle over the Canadian identity: are we stronger because of our cultural diversity, or weakened by institutionalizing it? It's been marred at times by charges of racism on one side and misrepresentation on the other, invective, catcalls and telephoned threats to trustees. Callers have also harassed board staff. *(Toronto Star, 1982, May 4, A16)*

Letters to the editor have reflected the strong opposition felt by many people to any expansion of heritage language teaching, as recommended by the Work Group on Third Language Instruction of the Toronto Board (1982). One correspondent (Joan Lynn) in a May 1982 issue of the *Toronto Star* pointed out that many immigrants "are quietly preserving their own language in their homes and circles of friendship" and went on to suggest that "it is unlikely that there is spare money around for this luxury, unless we are all willing to pay higher taxes." Similar financial concerns were expressed in a letter by Barbara Stuart (*Toronto Star,* May, 1982): "Surely from a financial standpoint, there is a matter of priorities here. If so much as a single dollar extra can be found in any budget for implementation of the Third Language Report, should that dollar not be spent on the more urgent of our problems?" Another correspondent (Steve Gurion, *Toronto Star,* May, 1982) asked "How are these ethnic children ever going to integrate and assimilate into the Canadian culture stream if they do not possess English?"

The case against teaching heritage languages within the school day was succinctly put by Marion Hausman, president of the Deer Park School Association, in a submission to the Toronto Board:

> Many people of diverse backgrounds fear balkanization of school communities, loss of time for core curriculum subjects, undue pressure on children, disruption in school programming and staffing, inadequate preparation for eventual employment, and indeed, a dramatic shift of direction in Canadian society.
> *(cited in Johnson, 1982)*

Some of the most extreme rhetoric on heritage languages during this period was penned by Judi McLeod the Toronto Sun's education columnist who, in one column, depicted some parents who were lobbying for heritage language programs as "diabolical as any of the characters from the imaginative pen of Charles Dickens ... a nasty lot indeed" (quoted in Barber, 1988, p. 53). In a similar vein she objected to a private member's bill introduced by Tony Grande in the Ontario Legislature that would have enabled heritage languages to be taught during the regular school day:

I call the bill hogwash. The nauseating strategy of the lib-left will undoubtedly see any who speak against the heritage-language bill branded as racists and bigots. Yet educators keep telling us that one of the most pressing educational problems is the number of students graduating from high schools without an adequate grasp of English. *(Toronto Sun, January 19, 1987, p. 18)*

The most recent heritage language controversy in Metropolitan Toronto resulted from the Ontario government's legislation, announced in October 1988, forcing school boards to offer the program when requested to do so by parents of 25 or more elementary school students enrolled with the board. This move was primarily directed against the Scarborough Board of Education that had adamantly refused to implement the program despite strong pressure from community groups for more than a decade. In the debate leading up to this legislation the opposing positions were clearly expressed once again in letters to the editor. In the *Toronto Star* (October 3, 1987), Pamela Kirk expressed the case for the opposition as follows:

Bringing our children up with the knowledge of their cultural background would make them more tolerable [sic] of other cultures and beliefs. Right? Not exactly. The new proposals to implement Heritage Language Education in Scarborough would do exactly the opposite. In teaching children about individual cultural backgrounds and ideologies, we would be separating them from the right to their Canadian identity. ... A knowledge of one's cultural background should stem from the home, in which it is the job of the parents to teach their children. The job should not be left up to a board of education that doesn't have enough money in its budget to replace books that are missing pages ...or that can't afford to repair a few clarinets with missing keys. *(Toronto Star, October 3, 1987)*

On the same page the Multicultural and Race Relations Committee of Human Services of Scarborough presented diametrically opposed arguments in an open letter to Premier Peterson:

Mr. Premier, you are no doubt well aware of the many benefits that flow from the mastery and proficiency of more than one language; not just in economic terms, but also a psychological sense of accomplishment and a sense of identity and pride in one's ancestral roots — without giving up or compromising one's identity and pride as a Canadian first and foremost. *(Toronto Star, October 3, 1987)*

Although the Ontario debate has been by far the most divisive, other provinces have also experienced public controversy over the heritage languages issue. In Quebec, for example, the Programme d'Enseignement des Langues et des Cultures d'Origine (PELCO)[2] provides heritage language instruction for approximately 100 hours per school year for the most part outside the regular school timetable but in some cases within regular school hours. This program has expanded considerably in recent years but is still on a much smaller scale than the Ontario Heritage Languages Program (approximately 5,000 students compared to more than 90,000 in the Ontario program in 1986/87). Controversy broke out in 1982 over the proposal to offer an Arabic language course in a French public school in the Montreal suburb of St. Laurent. Francophone parents overwhelmingly rejected the proposed program. As reported in the *Globe and Mail* (November 22, 1982, C10):

Suzanne Turgeon, a mother of two, led the vote against PELO because she felt it was a 'luxury program' in times of Government cutbacks. Mrs. Turgeon said she would rather see her children receive English language teaching than have the money spent on heritage languages. ... 'I'm not against multiculturalism,' Mrs. Turgeon stressed, 'but I don't want to see my money going to the Arabic community. If anything I want more English taught in this province.'

Clearly, the debate on heritage languages goes far beyond the benefits or otherwise of language teaching, as such. What is being contested is the nature of Canadian identity and the perceived self-interest of different sectors of Canadian society. While the dominant anglophone and francophone groups generally are strongly in favour of learning the other official language, they see few benefits to promoting heritage languages for themselves, for Canadian society as a whole, or for children from ethnocultural backgrounds. The educational focus for such children should be on acquiring English and becoming Canadian rather than on erecting linguistic and cultural barriers between them and their Canadian peers. In short, whereas advocates of heritage language teaching stress the value of bilingual and multilingual skills for the individual and society as a whole, opponents see heritage languages as socially divisive, excessively costly, and educationally retrograde in view of minority children's need to succeed academically in the school language.

The political debates on heritage language teaching do not fall neatly into traditional categories of left wing versus right wing. Witness the fact that one of the most consistent supporters of expanded opportunities for heritage language instruction at the Toronto Board has been Alexander Chumak, noted for strongly conservative views on most other issues considered by the Board. Chumak was Vice-Chairperson of The Work Group on Third Language Instruction in the Toronto Board whose March 1982 report occasioned the vehement opposition sketched above. The Chairperson of the Work Group was NDP trustee, Antonio Silipo, whose political orientation on most issues (except heritage languages) is diametrically opposed to Chumak's. Another indication of the political complexity of the issue is the fact that conservative governments in the Prairie provinces have initiated and strongly supported full bilingual programs involving heritage languages (50% English, 50% heritage language). In fact, Alberta and, in particular, the Edmonton Public School System, pioneered bilingual programs from the early 1970's involving Ukrainian, German, Hebrew, Yiddish, Polish, Chinese, and Arabic. By contrast, the Liberal government in Ontario has continued the policy of its conservative predecessor by refusing to permit instruction through the medium of any language other than English and French, except for short-term transitional purposes.[3]

Similarly, the issues are not fully reducible to a conflict between the interests of the anglophone and francophone dominant groups and those of less politically influential ethnocultural groups.[4] Although most of the opposition to heritage language teaching has been voiced by members of the dominant groups, some members of ethnocultural communities have also expressed concerns that efforts at language maintenance are ill-advised and that newcomers should strive to be Canadians first.

In subsequent chapters we will analyze the issues underlying the opposing positions in this debate. Clearly, the perennial question of what constitutes and who defines the Canadian identity is central. We examine this issue in the next chapter and attempt to put the heritage language controversy in historical perspective. The third chapter examines how federal and provincial multicultural policies evolved to include heritage language promotion. We trace the beginnings of this policy evolution from Book IV of the Bilingualism and Biculturalism Commission through the federally-commissioned attitude studies of the 1970's to the cautious policy initiatives that provided some government funding for community efforts in language promotion. The escalation of controversy in the 1980's is also described in some detail. Chapter 4 examines the rationale for heritage language promotion in the public school system. We argue that the languages of Canadian children are human resources that have significance for children's individual psychological and educational development and for Canadian society as a whole. The fifth chapter examines one special minority language context, that of the Deaf community, in order to illustrate aspects of the educational rationale for heritage language instruction. The final chapter compares Canadian heritage language provision with developments in other countries and outlines alternative directions for developing Canada's linguistic resources and responding to the rapidly changing realities of our global community.

FOOTNOTES

[1] The term "heritage language" usually refers to all languages other than the aboriginal languages of Native and Inuit peoples and the "official" Canadian languages (English and French). A variety of other terms have been used in Canada to refer to heritage languages: for example, "ethnic," "minority," "ancestral," "third," and "non-official" have all been used at different times and in different provinces. The term used in Quebec is "langues d'origine." In other countries the term "community languages" is used (e.g. Australia, Britain, New Zealand) and the term "mother-tongue teaching" is also common. A number of Canadian proponents of heritage language teaching have expressed misgivings about the term because it connotes learning about past traditions rather than acquiring language skills that have significance for children's overall educational and personal development. In the Toronto Board of Education the term "modern languages" is used partly in an attempt to defuse the strong emotional reactions that the term "heritage languages" evokes.

[2] The program was originally termed "Projet d'Enseignement des Langues d'Origine" [PELO].

[3] The issue of mother-tongue teaching for minority students has confounded "left-right" political distinctions in many countries during the past 20 years. For example, in France the teaching of regional languages such as Provençal, Breton, and Catalan was for many years viewed by the left as an affront to the ideals of the Republic and as a right-wing Catholic plot. This view has changed somewhat in the last decade. Similarly, in Germany left-wing educators strongly opposed separate mother-tongue schools for children of migrant workers (as in the Bavarian model) on the grounds that these were intended to prevent integration into German society. By contrast, in Sweden, the Finnish minority with the support of labour unions and left-wing academics has successfully argued the case for mother-tongue medium instruction, through elementary school and beyond, as a prerequisite for children's academic and cognitive development and ultimate participation in both Swedish and Finnish societies. For an insightful review of these apparent contradictions see Skutnabb-Kangas (1984).

[4] We are using the term "ethnocultural" to refer to the subset of Canadian ethnic communities that come from backgrounds other than those of the official language groups and aboriginal groups. Our use of the term does not imply that anglophone, francophone, and aboriginal groups are not also characterized by "ethnicity."

Chapter 2

Lifting the Multicultural Veil
The Manufacture of Canadian Identity

Introduction

Harold Troper (1979) has argued cogently that multiculturalism has come to play a role in filling an "identity vacuum"
among English Canadians brought about by the gradual
demise of Anglo-conformity. Thus, Canadians tend to view
themselves as always having been tolerant of ethnic and cultural diversity and speak derisively of the American "melting
pot" as representing a societal attitude far less enlightened than
the Canadian "mosaic." The possibility of racism among
Canadians is denied in the popular consciousness by a powerful set of images ranging from the "underground railroad" for
Black slaves escaping from the United States to the colourful
celebration of multicultural festivals at regular intervals across
the country.

We argue in this chapter that the incorporation of "celebratory multiculturalism" into the national psyche is largely a superficial window-dressing exercise that serves both psychological
and political functions for both the general public and policy-
makers. Despite the genuine efforts of many policy-makers
and the positive intent of a large number of Canadians, racist
institutional structures are very much in evidence behind the
multicultural facade. This is particularly so with respect to the
issue of public support for the development of Canada's lin-

guistic resources. We first consider the historical reality, relying primarily on Troper's analysis, and then examine some concrete illustrations of the way institutionalized racism continues to operate in the daily workings of schools. The continued operation of these racist structures suggests that the major changes that have occurred in "multicultural rhetoric" during the past 20 years are not matched by coherent and consistent strategies to transform this rhetoric into reality.

Multiculturalism and the Canadian Identity

The prevailing attitude towards ethnic diversity in English Canada during the first part of this century was that ethnic groups should give up their own languages and cultures and become assimilated to the dominant British group. This Anglo-conformity orientation is well expressed by a speaker to the 1913 Presbyterian Pre-Assembly Congress in Toronto:

> The problem is simply this: take all the different nationalities, German, French, Italian, Russian and all the others that are sending their surplus into Canada: mix them with the Anglo-Saxon stock and produce a uniform race wherein the Anglo-Saxon peculiarities shall prevail *(quoted by Harney & Troper, 1975, p. 110).*

Education was naturally regarded as a major means of Canadianizing "foreign" students. Harney and Troper (1975) point out that Canadianization was not a hidden curriculum but permeated every facet of the school program. Any traces of foreign values were to be eradicated in the process of impressing on students the Canadian values of "punctuality, regularity, obedience, industry, cleanliness, decency of appearance and behaviour, regard for the rights of others and respect for law and order" (p. 110).

Surveys of the views of Canadian educators in the early part of the century (Black, 1913; Sissons, 1917; Anderson, 1918) emphasized the desirability of rapid assimilation and the necessity to eradicate students' first language (L1) in order to facilitate the learning of English and acquisition of Canadian values. Black, for example, concluded that

> Generally speaking ...it is evident that the wisest method of teaching English will aim at eliminating for the time being

from the learner's consciousness all memory or thought of his vernacular tongue (1913, p. 106).

Of all Canadian minority groups, Native students experienced the most brutal suppression of language and culture in residential schools. Separated from their families for years, severely punished for speaking Native languages, and taught that Native culture and religion were beneath contempt, Native students frequently emerged from these schools with their language and culture destroyed and their sense of self-worth eradicated. These schools continued to operate until the 1980s.

In Cape Breton, Gaelic was similarly suppressed during the latter part of the 19th century and well into the present century. Shaw (1983) estimates that at its peak there were probably about 100,000 speakers of Gaelic as a first language in Cape Breton but the educational policies pursued in the local schools had a devastating effect on the language.

> The attitude of educators towards Gaelic was a faithful copy of the policies in effect in the British Isles. The main rule was that Gaelic was not allowed in the schoolhouse, though everyone present, including the teacher, often as not had a far deeper knowledge of Gaelic than could be equalled by the rudimentary school English of those times. The policy was pursued to the point where people living today remember being physically punished at school for using Gaelic (1983, p. 74).

Watson (1988) similarly notes that Gaelic home culture was not, and still is not, perceived as worthy of inclusion in the core curriculum of the schools.

The current endorsement of multiculturalism as national and provincial policy tends to obscure the strong assimilationist orientation of Canadian educators in the past and the racist character of much of our public policy throughout this century. For example, between 1885, when a head tax was imposed on Chinese immigrants and 1967, Canada pursued a 'whites only' immigration policy. Other examples of our racist past include:

◆ The treatment of Blacks in the Maritimes and Ontario who were educated predominantly in segregated schools during most of the 19th and 20th centuries (Ashworth, 1988). The last separate Black school in Ontario was closed in 1965;

◆ The exclusion of Jews before and during the second world war (Abella and Troper, 1984);

◆ The treatment of Japanese-Canadians during the second world war;

◆The continuing failure to alleviate the deplorable conditions under which many Native Canadians live (e.g. infant mortality 60% higher than the national rate) and to reverse the widespread school failure of Native students (e.g. 80% drop-out rate compared to 25% for other Canadians).

Despite our racist past, as Canadians we still tend to view ourselves as always having been a more tolerant and open society than our neighbours to the south. As expressed by Troper (1979):

> Perhaps every country needs its myths and national cliches. For English speaking Canada one current and often repeated cliche is that Canada owes its distinctive character to a long fostered tolerance of cultural diversity—we are a mosaic while the Americans are a melting pot. According to this vision we have always had an unofficial multicultural policy and [the declaration of this policy in] 1971 only made official what Canadians had long accepted as well and true. ... If anything the opposite is closer to the truth. The survival of active and distinct ethnic communities in Canada, especially before World War II, occurred in spite of public policy and sentiment not because of them. ... Ethnicity, if tolerated at all, was seen as a temporary stage through which one passed on the road to full assimilation. Prolonged ethnic identification ... was seen as a pathological condition to be overcome, not as a source of national enrichment and pride (1979, p. 9).

Troper goes on to point out that many Canadians decried the American melting pot metaphor on the grounds that the racial and ethnic mixing implied by the melting pot seemed dangerous at best:

> The melting pot, they felt, carried to its fullest extent, preached racial mongrelization and an end to accepted public morality. ...Instead, Anglo-Canadians demanded one-sided change and only on the part of the immigrant. The object was to change *them* to *us* as closely, quickly and cheaply as possible. The foreigner need not actually mix with Anglo-Canadians, he must just behave as if this had been the case. (1979, p. 9-10).

With the gradual weakening of the ties to Britain after the second world war and the virtual disappearance of the British Empire, it was unclear to what extent Canadians had an identity distinct from that of Americans. Troper suggests that "multiculturalism" has come to fill that identity vacuum and, in the process mythologized Canadians' historical treatment of immigrant groups:

> Thus, multiculturalism, filling the identity vacuum left in the wake of World War II, made yesterday's vices into today's virtues. Rather than lament the failure of Anglo-conformity and assault the continuity of ethnicity as a demonic threat to cohesion, as an earlier generation would surely have done, the new policy proudly champions the mosaic. Furthermore the survival of ethnic identity in Canada, as in the United States, in spite of the best efforts of past educators and other guardians of the gate, is now toasted as that unique element in the Canadian cultural pattern which assures Canada of a separate character from the United States. *(Cummins and Troper, 1985, p. 20)*

The current rhetoric of multiculturalism, however, is frequently at variance with the continuing underground reality of Anglo-conformity. Given the relative recency of an official multiculturalism policy and the strong Anglo-conformity tradition that preceded it, it is hardly surprising that assimilationist orientations are still prominent in many Canadian institutions, including schools. Michael Valpy (1989) notes that in public opinion polls a majority of Canadians has always responded affirmatively when asked whether Canada accepts too many immigrants, and currently public anxiety about immigration and racism is at its highest point in Canadian polling history. Blatant discrimination against non-white applicants in housing and jobs has been demonstrated repeatedly in studies conducted during the 1980's in cities such as Toronto and Montreal (for reviews of these studies see *Currents,* Vol. 5, No. 2, April 1989).

One cause for optimism, however, is that government agencies have begun to acknowledge the extent of racism in Canadian society and to establish a legal infrastructure to promote human rights (e.g. the Employment Equity Act, the Canadian Charter of Rights and Freedoms, and the Canadian Multiculturalism Act). Gerry Weiner, the Minister of State for

Multiculturalism and Citizenship, recently highlighted problems of racism in Canadian society in perhaps a more candid manner than any previous federal Minister:

> We have to face up to what the researchers and the evidence tell us; that almost a third of our population—not just one university professor—actually believes in the theory of racial superiority. That some 15 per cent or so of our population practices open racial discrimination. Imbalance and under-representation do not exist only in our police forces. Prejudice, discrimination and the virtual exclusion of visible minorities and Native Canadians have been the standard procedure in much of Canadian life for just about as long as anyone has been keeping records. Is there one valid reason why, in this year 1989, 40 years after the universal declaration of human rights, Blacks are turned down three times as often as Whites when looking for rental accommodation? Or why a Black applicant is offered only one job for every three offered a White? (1989, p. 4)

Weiner went on to identify racial myths that are common in Canadian society; for example, the myth that Aboriginal Canadians are unreliable and lazy, that they are not capable of managing their own affairs; the myth that Blacks are more prone to criminal activity than other people; the myth that East Asians adhere to alien and incomprehensible cultures and values in preference to Canadian ways and values; the myth that immigrants cause racism because they take jobs away from hard-working Canadians or live on social assistance which has to be paid for by hard-working Canadians (1989, p. 6). All of these myths are refuted by the empirical evidence (e.g. see *Currents*, Vol 5, No. 2, April 1989) but they operate to create systemic racism in many Canadian institutions.

The complexities of translating rhetoric into reality are illustrated in the Minister's acknowledgement that Native Canadians have been subject to the most extreme racism of any group in Canada. In pointing out that immigration does not cause racism he noted that "the one group in our society which has been discriminated against more persistently and systematically than any other is the one group in our society which has not come from elsewhere—our Native peoples" (p. 15). The irony here is that less than two weeks later, the Assembly of First Nations took out a full page in the *Globe and Mail* (April 4, 1989, A11) to write an open letter to the Prime Minister to protest against federal government cutbacks for Native post-secondary education and reduction of Native economic development expenditures. During the same period Native students went on an extended hunger strike in Ottawa to protest the cutbacks in post-secondary opportunities for Native students. Racial minorities are also underrepresented to a major extent in the federal public service.

In summary, most Canadians have internalized the myth that Canada, unlike our American neighbours, has always had a tradition of openness to immigrants and tolerance of other cultures. The Canadian mosaic has stood in shining contrast to the American melting pot. In reality, Canada has a tradition of racism against Native peoples, Blacks and Asians that is comparable to that of the United States and other western countries (e.g. Britain, Australia, New Zealand, etc). The adoption of multicultural policies at federal, provincial and local levels of government is clearly a positive step in reversing this tradition of racism. Multicultural policies, however, are double-edged in that by celebrating superficial aspects of cultural diversity (e.g. ethnic food and festivals) they can deflect attention away from subtle and still very powerful forms of institutional racism. Thus, the myth that Canada has always been tolerant of cultural and racial diversity is reinforced by superficial displays of "celebratory multiculturalism" in schools and elsewhere.

The vehemence of the negative reaction to heritage language instruction in the public school system can be understood in the context of the persistence of Anglo-conformity (or, under very different conditions, Franco-conformity in Quebec) in the minds and hearts of many Canadians. Thus, while "multiculturalism" contributes a surface veneer to Canadian identity, at a deeper level, in English Canada, identity is still largely rooted in Anglo-conformity. The proclamation of "multiculturalism" as both Canadian policy and Canadian identity, while acting as a catalyst for many worthwhile policies and initiatives, has served to obscure the continuing reality of racist assumptions and traditions among a major segment of the Canadian population.[1]

Language and Institutionalized Discrimination in Canadian Schools

The term "institutionalized discrimination" refers to systematic forms of unequal treatment or division of resources between societal groups defined on the basis of race, sex, language or social class that are legitimized by individual belief systems or institutional structures and procedures (e.g. educational assessment practices). In other words, the discrimination is brought about both by the ways particular institutions such as schools are organized or structured and by the (usually) implicit assumptions that legitimize that organization. For example, the over-representation of Black students in Basic level programs at the secondary level in several Metropolitan Toronto boards of education can be analyzed as a function of institutionalized racism in the educational system (see for example, Wright and Tsuji, 1984).

We argue that despite the advent of multicultural education policies in school systems across Canada, institutionalized discrimination continues to operate in the educational system to discourage students from developing competence in their heritage language. The structures that promote institutionalized discrimination in the area of heritage languages include the following:

◆ Legal prohibition or constraints on the use of heritage languages as languages of instruction in some provinces (e.g. Ontario);

◆ Legal constraints on the extent to which heritage languages can be legitimized educationally by being taught within the regular school day;

◆ Absence of structures whereby heritage language teachers can obtain in-service training and accreditation for the teaching of heritage languages;

◆ Omission of issues relating to minority students' bilingualism and processes of language learning from both the teacher accreditation courses offered by Faculties of Education and from graduate courses pursued by psychoeducational consultants and other special educators; the result is the perpetuation of incorrect belief systems that promote discriminatory practices; for example, advising minority parents to switch to English as the language of communication in the home.

These discriminatory structures are supported by a variety of beliefs regarding language development among minority students that have not changed substantially in recent years. These include:

◆ The belief that bilingualism is a negative force in the educational development of minority children;

◆ The belief that use of the heritage language in the home will impede children's learning of English and overall academic progress;

◆ The belief that heritage language instruction and/or bilingual education involving heritage languages will retard children's academic progress;

◆ The belief that non-standard varieties of English or French (e.g. Caribbean Creoles) are inferior to the standard forms and should not be tolerated in the classroom;[2]

◆ The belief that standardized IQ and achievement tests are culturally and linguistically appropriate for minority students as soon as they can speak English fluently (usually within about two years of beginning to learn English).

The lists of structures and belief systems could be extended considerably but these are the major issues that we will consider in subsequent chapters. At this point we will examine just one example of how these structures and belief systems operate to discriminate against minority students in order to illustrate how institutional structures can remain firmly rooted in Anglo-conformity despite a superficial adherence to the goals of multicultural education.

Institutionalized Discrimination and Psychological Assessment of Minority Students

The training of every Canadian psychoeducational consultant includes reference to the possibility of cultural bias in standardized IQ tests and to the fact that in the late sixties it was found that there were about 3-4 times as many Black and Hispanic students in the United States in classes for the educable mentally retarded as would be expected on the basis of their proportion in the school population. This over-representation is usually attributed to the combined effect of discriminatory school practices and discriminatory assessment. The items on typical IQ tests reflect the experiences and values of middle-class White students and exclude any knowledge that minority students (usually working-class) may have gained as a result of experiences typical or unique to their culture. These tests also tap forms of reasoning that are more likely to be taught explicitly in middle-class than in working-class families (see Cummins, 1984 for a detailed discussion of standardized tests and minority students). The following items from the *Wechsler Intelligence Test for Children—Revised Edition (WISC-R)* (1974) illustrate the kinds of knowledge that is legitimized on such tests:

Who discovered America?

How tall is the average Canadian man?

What are you supposed to do if you find someone's wallet or purse in a store?

Why is it usually better to give money to a well-known charity than to a street beggar?

The cultural and social class bias of such items is obvious; yet this test continues to be administered to minority children across Canada every day and decisions about whether the child is retarded, learning disabled, or of "normal" ability are made on the basis of this type of measure. Research has shown that on the Information subtest (from which the first two items above are taken) children from non-English home backgrounds scored considerably lower than expected norms (Cummins, 1984); specifically, 70% of the sample of ESL students scored 6 or below on this subtest compared to only 16% of the test norming sample and more than a third (34%) of the ESL sample scored 3 or below compared to only 2.5% of the test norming sample. A similar pattern of very low performance was found on most of the other verbal subtests.

Despite the fact that Canadian policy-makers and educators are very familiar with the American data on the virtual inevitability of bias against minority students on verbal IQ tests, the issue has received minimal attention. The issue has scarcely been raised in Canadian academic journals during the past decade and Ministries of Education have largely ignored the issue until very recently. The implicit assumption appears to be that racism and other forms of discrimination against minorities are American problems and such concerns are not relevant to Canadian education.

The development of special education policy in Ontario illustrates this selective screening out of equity concerns despite the loud endorsement of multicultural education policies at various levels of the educational hierarchy. During the late seventies and early eighties, Ontario phased in Bill 82, modelled on the U.S. law PL94-142, which required school boards to identify all exceptional students (e.g. gifted, learning disabled, etc) and provide them with an education appropriate to their needs. As a result of litigation in the early seventies, school districts in the United States were required to take steps to correct abuses of standardized tests and some non-discriminatory assessment provisions were built into PL94-142. Specifically, students were required to be assessed in their primary language unless it was clearly not feasible to do so. Throughout the seventies and early eighties, psychological and special education journals in the United States printed numerous articles on issues related to assessment of minority students.

Yet the issue of non-discriminatory assessment is virtually ignored in Bill 82 and in supporting documentation. Vague cautions are given to the effect that "where a child's language is other than English or French, a reasonable delay in the language-based aspects of assessment should be considered" (Ministry of Education, 1980, p. 5). However, no suggestions are given as to what constitutes a "reasonable delay" nor are pitfalls associated with the use of IQ tests with minority students discussed.[3]

The fact that Ontario policy-makers appear not to have even considered the possibility that psychological tests might discriminate against minority students (despite overwhelming evidence from the United States of the cultural and linguistic biases of such tests) shows how irrelevant the rhetoric of multiculturalism is to the day-to-day functioning of the educational system. Radically different implementation procedures would have resulted if policy-makers and educators had seriously acknowledged the province's cultural and linguistic diversity. It would have been necessary to ensure that psychoeducational consultants were knowledgeable about issues related to bilingualism, cultural diversity, and approaches to non-discriminatory assessment. For example, the research data showing that typical verbal IQ tests seriously underestimate minority students' academic potential for up to five years after starting to learn English (Cummins, 1984) would have necessitated a radical rethinking of assessment procedures. And of course, the class bias in these tests is evident even after the majority language has been acquired. It would also have been difficult to evade the obvious desirability of involving heritage language instructors (or other speakers of heritage languages) in the assessment process so that students' conceptual development in their first language could be estimated.

In short, it appears to have been more convenient to ignore the issue of bias against minority students in assessment practices than to deal with it. Despite the veneer of "multicultural education" policies at both ministry and school board level, there is little evidence that psychological assessment practices are significantly more equitable today than they were in the heyday of Anglo-conformity. Undoubtedly, most psychoeducational consultants are increasingly sensitive to the issue of testing bias but, for the most part, they operate in a broader institutional structure that still does not acknowledge the population changes that have taken place and their implications for the entire special education enterprise. No structure has been established to ensure that psychoeducational consultants and other educators are knowledgeable about research on bilingualism in the home and school and fully realize the limitations of typical standardized tests for use with minority students. The rhetoric of "multicultural education" has been neatly sidestepped so that the status quo is left largely unchallenged.

Conclusion

During the past two decades Canadians have come to view the notion of multiculturalism as characteristically Canadian, a dimension of our identity that distinguishes us from Americans. Thus, racial intolerance and systemic discrimination against minority groups are seen, at one level of our consciousness, as American issues that are not problematic in the Canadian context. The celebration of multiculturalism in its superficial aspects has contributed to two patently false views of Canadian society: (a) that we have always been tolerant and open towards minorities, and (b) that currently there is little or no discrimination against minorities in Canadian institutions. The reality is that Canadian belief systems and institutional structures (including schools) have always been just as racist as those in other western countries and institutional discrimination against minorities on the basis of race, language and culture continues to exist, although in less overt form than in previous times. In the educational system this process of institutional discrimination is clearly illustrated in procedures for psychological assessment of minority students.

The orientation of Canadian educators and policy-makers in most provinces towards heritage language education displays a similar disjunction between a surface-level endorsement of heritage language teaching as one aspect of multicultural education and a more deep-rooted rejection of such programs as a potential threat to the societal status quo, specifically the primacy of English and/or French as the languages of power in Canadian society. Commentators typically have no objection to communities teaching heritage languages quietly in their own homes or community schools, but they object strenuously to heritage language teaching being institutionalized within the public school system and supported by public monies.

We shall argue in subsequent chapters that educational considerations are routinely subordinated to political considerations in devising policies and programs to promote heritage language teaching. This, in itself, is not surprising. However, it is symptomatic of the lack of imagination that has characterized the implementation of this central aspect of Canada's much-vaunted multiculturalism policy in most parts of the country. Rather than providing incentives for schools and communities to explore collaboratively a variety of innovative ways of responding to Canada's linguistic diversity and developing children's minds, myopic politicians have legislated educators to remain in their shells and concentrate on producing "solid citizens." Where children have developed trilingualism, it has usually been in spite of the school system rather than because of it. The primacy of political considerations in the heritage language debate obscures the fact that there is no educational reason why all Canadian children should not leave school at least trilingual; however, as a society we choose, for the most part, not to pursue this course because to do so would legitimize the knowledge, values and languages of ethnocultural groups who are still regarded as subordinate in Canadian society; the brittle remnants of Anglo-conformity would be further weakened by any intrusion of heritage languages into mainstream Canadian institutions.

FOOTNOTES

[1] Many social scientists have pointed to the lack of conceptual clarity surrounding multiculturalism and multicultural education. Mallea (1989), for example, raises the following issues;

> Are multiculturalism and multicultural education socio-political instruments for ensuring cooperation by the granting of limited concessions? Are they designed to realize democratic ideals or are they another form of social control? Do multicultural education policies assume knowledge will reduce prejudice and discrimination? Do they recognize and legitimize cultural differences while failing to deal with racism at the institutional, structural and individual level? Or, as some argue, do current approaches help maintain the myth about subordinate groups as 'problems to be studied', while leaving institutional and structural inequalities intact? (p. 114)

[2] See Ramphal 1983, 1985, for excellent discussions of how teachers' misconceptions about Caribbean Creole can jeopardize children's development of reading ability.

[3] The issue has received somewhat greater Ministry of Education attention in recent years but few concrete initiatives have resulted to date (see Samuda et al [1989]).

Chapter 3

The Ambivalent Embrace
From Multiculturalism to Multilingualism

The rise of Quebec nationalism and separatist sentiment led the federal government to establish the Royal Commission on Bilingualism and Biculturalism (the B & B Commission) in 1963

> ...to inquire into and report upon the existing state of bilingualism and biculturalism in Canada and to recommend what steps should be taken to develop the Canadian Confederation on the basis of an equal partnership between the two founding races, taking into account the contribution of the other ethnic groups to the enrichment of Canada and the measures that should be taken to safeguard that contribution. (1966, p. 151)

The "other ethnic groups," particularly those of Ukrainian descent, strongly pressed the case that multiculturalism should be central to the Canadian identity. The B & B Commission accepted this view and on October 8, 1971, Prime Minister Trudeau proclaimed the policy of "multiculturalism within a bilingual framework" under which there are two official languages but no official culture and no ethnic group takes precedence over any other.

Book IV of the B & B Commission report made explicit the value of linguistic diversity to Canada as a whole:

> The presence in Canada of many people whose language and culture are distinctive by reason of their birth or ancestry represents an inestimable enrichment that Canadians can not afford to lose. The dominant culture can only profit from the influence of these other cultures. Linguistic variety is unquestionably an advantage and its beneficial effects on the country are priceless. (1970, p. 14)

The Commission recommended that educators explore ways of promoting the development of these linguistic resources but cautioned that promotion of heritage languages should not be at the expense of French or English.

In the early seventies, policy-makers attempted to define more precisely what specific policies and programs were implied by the general endorsement of multiculturalism. In particular, the relationship of multiculturalism to the promotion of non-official languages was unclear. While ethnocultural groups urged that "culture" without language represented little more than an empty shell and multilingualism in some form was implied by multiculturalism, others cautioned that promotion of languages other than English and French would erect barriers between cultural groups and, in effect, represent the antithesis of multiculturalism.

While ethnocultural groups, by and large, acclaimed the multiculturalism policy, some commentators pointed to the "persistent ambiguities" in the policy. Lupul (1981) for example, describes the policy as "a piece of political pragmatism" which

> ...pleased no one who considered the policy seriously. The failure to provide multiculturalism with a linguistic base especially displeased the Ukrainians; the loosening of the ties between language and culture angered the francophones who disliked any suggestion that the status of their culture was on a par with that of other ethnic groups. (1981, pp. 12-13)

In order to test the political ground with respect to multiculturalism and multilingualism, the federal government commissioned two large-scale national surveys: the *Non-Official Languages Study* (O'Bryan, Reitz & Kuplowska, 1976) and the *Majority Attitudes Study* (Berry, Kalin & Taylor, 1977).

The *Non-Official Languages Study* showed that among ten ethnic groups surveyed, a large majority of individuals were committed to ethnic language maintenance for their children and felt that public institutional support was needed if this goal was to be achieved. The study also provided very clear evidence of rapid language loss across generations; in fact, language loss was mentioned most often as the major problem facing the ethnic group, by comparison with problems such as job discrimination or educational opportunities. O'Bryan et al reported "very strong and clear support among many members of Canada's ethnic minority groups for inclusion of the non-official languages in the courses of instruction and as vehicles of instruction in the public schools—especially in the elementary schools" (1976, p. 176). While many respondents felt that the prime responsibility for language maintenance lay with parents, O'Bryan et al point out that the rapid intergenerational loss of language indicates that the task is not being successfully borne by parents. They suggest, in fact, that "the job of preserving language is quite possibly beyond them" (1976, p. 176).

The *Majority Attitudes Study* showed that Canadians of English and French backgrounds were mildly positive towards the idea of cultural diversity; however, there was considerably more support for manifestations of cultural diversity such as ethnic festivals, community centres, etc., than there was for teaching heritage languages in regular school programs or for broadcasting in heritage languages. In fact, respondents showed slight rejection of the last two programs. There was strong early rejection of the notion of "multiculturalism" from some Quebec academics and policy-makers who saw it as a ploy to reduce the status of their culture to just one among many minority cultures dominated by Anglo-Canadians (e.g. Rocher, 1973).

Despite the opposition from Quebec to the notion of multiculturalism, the two national surveys were interpreted as supporting multicultural initiatives that were already underway in areas such as ethnic studies, intercultural communication, performing arts, etc. The *Non-Official Languages Study* was also influential in the establishment in June 1977 of the Multiculturalism Directorate's Cultural Enrichment Program whereby support is provided to ethnocultural communities for the teaching of heritage languages. Parallel support programs for community-operated heritage language programs and for heritage language bilingual programs in the public schools were already operating in the prairie provinces at the time the Cultural Enrichment Program was established, and in the same month the Ontario government announced the Ontario Heritage Languages program. By this time also, the provincial government in Quebec was supporting the teaching of heritage languages both in community-run schools and in regular school programs as part of their policy initiatives in the area of "interculturalism," a construct intended to promote acceptance and communication between cultural groups without necessarily implying that all cultural groups are equal.

Thus, by 1977, despite the ambivalence of many anglophone and francophone Canadians, the federal government and some provincial governments had taken initial steps to endorse heritage language promotion as a component of their multicultural policies.

Support for heritage language teaching has gradually expanded during the past decade at both federal and provincial levels of government, although the pace has been slower than many advocates would like. At a federal level, the Canada Multiculturalism Act was enshrined in law in 1988 and the Canadian Heritage Languages Institute will be established in Edmonton by 1990 with large-scale funding.[1] The numbers of students enrolled in community-operated supplementary heritage language schools has continued to increase since the Cultural Enrichment Program was first announced in 1977. Multiculturalism Minister Gerry Weiner, in announcing the establishment of the Heritage Languages Institute in September 1989, noted that there are currently 129,000 students studying 60 languages in supplementary schools across the country .

At a provincial level, the major developments in heritage language teaching provision have occurred in Quebec, Ontario, and the Prairie provinces. The situation in these provinces will be reviewed first followed by consideration of developments in the Atlantic provinces and British Columbia.[2]

The Evolution of
Heritage Language Programs in Quebec

During the past decade, public attention to this question both in Quebec and in the rest of Canada has tended to be preoccupied with the issue of schooling rights for the Anglophone minority in the province. The education of other ethnic groups has become a public issue largely in the context of the English schools question. The passage of the Charter of the French Language (Bill 101) in 1977, largely restricted the right to attend English schools to children whose mother or father had received primary education through English in Quebec. This effectively barred most ethnic minority children from attendance at English schools. Not surprisingly, the protests from ethnic groups were vociferous and a substantial number of students (approximately 1,200 mainly of Italian background) continued to attend English schools in defiance of the law.

In recent years, more concern about the effects of Bill 101 has been voiced by the francophone community than by ethnocultural communities. Schools that formerly were largely attended by francophone students have suddenly become highly diverse both culturally and linguistically. Although French continues to be the only medium of instruction, a variety of other languages are spoken in the corridors and playgrounds. This is seen by some as a threat to Quebec culture and language maintenance. The adaptations of Quebec society to increasing diversity are likely to become more contentious as immigration increases to compensate for the extremely low birthrate in the province.

An indication of the potential tensions faced by the Quebec educational system comes from the controversy that arose from a survey of students and parents carried out by the Montreal Catholic School Commission which, in its initial version, included the following question: "Would you prefer that there be some schools for pure Québécois and others for ethnics, schools that are mixed half-and-half, or that things remain as they are?" The *Globe and Mail* reported the controversy as follows:

A Montreal Catholic school board survey that asks parents if they want 'ethnics' and 'pure Québécois' students segregated

27

in different schools has caused a furor among minority groups and academics. ... Education Minister Claude Ryan was ... quick to denounce the survey saying 'there is no such thing as different categories of Quebecers.' Jean Trottier, vice-president of the Montreal Catholic School Commission said the criticism was 'not justified' because 'it is not the intention of the commission to encourage xenophobia among respondents or to favor the establishment of segregated schools.' He said it would be ridiculous not to address the question of 'ethnics' in the school because it is an important issue. 'We do not want to avoid the ethnic aspect of our school system because it is an aspect that preoccupies parents,' Mr. Trottier said. *(Picard, 1989, p. A17).*

After much debate and national publicity the question was withdrawn from the survey.

The preoccupations of parents with respect to this issue will undoubtedly increase in view of the fact that the Quebec government is planning to increase its share of immigration to Canada to 25% from its traditional level of about 17%. This measure is being undertaken in order to halt the decline in the Quebec population resulting from the extremely low birthrate of 1.47 births per woman of child-bearing age (Malarek, 1989). In 1987, 27% of immigrants to Quebec spoke English only, 23% French only, 13% were bilingual in English and French and more than 36% spoke neither English or French. Malarek points to the adaptations that Quebec society is faced with as it confronts unprecedented cultural and linguistic diversity:

> But the prospect of increased immigration has also triggered debate in the province, with nationalists asserting that immigrants will dilute the old stock or 'Québécois de vieille souche'—a white, Catholic, francophone Quebecer with roots going back several generations. Although few will say so publicly, many acknowledge privately that increased immigration in the present climate is a recipe for racial disharmony—one that threatens the racial homogeneity of Quebec. (1989, p. A9)

According to Fo Niami, executive director of the Centre for Research Action on Race Relations in Montreal (cited in Malarek, 1989) there is some evidence that younger people are more open to cultural diversity so long as it does not express itself in English. He also noted that there is some contradiction in Quebec society "where on the one hand we have to integrate ethnic minorities and make them part of Quebec society, and on the other hand, we don't want them to be a full French Quebecer because of this attitude that 'we're here first and they came after'" (Malarek, 1989, p. A9). Ethnic leaders in Quebec also pointed to the contradiction between government policies of integrating minorities and the under-representation of ethnic minorities in institutions of power (e.g. while ethnic minorities represent 12% of the Quebec population, they account for only 4.3% of the province's civil service).

Despite the public ambivalence about cultural diversity and the primary focus on the English minority, there have been a considerable number of policy and program initiatives in relation to the education of ethnocultural groups in Quebec during the past decade. In 1981, the Government of Quebec published a plan of action for cultural communities, drawn up by the Ministry of Cultural Communities and Immigration, entitled "Autant de Façons d'Etre Québécois" (Quebecers Each and Every One). The major goals of this plan were as follows:

◆ To ensure the maintenance and development of the cultural communities as well as their uniqueness;

◆ To sensitize Quebec francophones to the contributions of the cultural communities to the common heritage of Quebec;

◆ To assist the cultural communities to integrate into Quebec society and particularly in those sectors where they have previously been underrepresented, such as the Public Service.

The aims of the Quebec concern with ethnocultural communities are made explicit in several documents. The affirmation of French as the common language of Quebec implies that steps be taken to help those who do not speak French acquire the language so that they can participate in the society as a whole. In the past, ethnic communities tended to orient themselves to the Anglophone sector partly because of the greater utility of English in North America but also because "they had been left aside by the Francophone milieu which had inherited a certain xenophobia from past struggles to survive"

(Government of Quebec, 1981, p. 10). Thus, the recent policies attempt to remove linguistic, cultural and racial barriers to integration and full participation while at the same time accepting the cultural realities of the ethnocultural communities.

Perhaps because of Quebec's own concern to safeguard the vitality of its language and culture, official documents reveal considerable sensitivity to and sympathy with the aspirations of ethnocultural communities in this respect; however, these documents also recognize that this perspective of acceptance is not shared by many Québécois who still do not consider immigrants to be "true Québécois" even after several generations. There is also insistence on the primacy of the French language and culture within Quebec. The point is made, for example, that rejection of the American "melting pot" concept does not imply that it is necessary

> ...for Quebec society to adopt the notion of multiculturalism as expressed by the 'Canadian mosaic' theory. The development of Quebec's cultural groups can be achieved through the collective vitality of the majority francophone society in much the same way that the trunk and roots of a tree nourish all its branches as well as any graftings. ... assimilation of the minority groups can be avoided if each and every one of them ... become conscious of their own original contribution to Quebec's cultural development. *(Gouvernement du Québec, Ministère des Communautés Culturelles et de l'Immigration, 1981, p. 12)*

Consistent with its declared pluralistic orientation, the Quebec government actively promotes the maintenance of heritage languages and cultures. There are three principal educational programs through which this is achieved: namely, support for private schools, the Programme d'Enseignement des Langues et des Cultures d'Origine (PELCO), and the Programme des Langues Ethniques (PLE).

Private Schools.

In Quebec there are close to 30 full-time private ethnic schools (mainly Jewish but also Greek and Armenian) which are subsidized for approximately 80% of their operating costs by the provincial government. These schools receive the same treatment as anglophone and francophone schools in the private sector. Research studies conducted within the Jewish school system suggest that these schools are highly effective in developing trilingual skills among their students (see Genesee, Tucker, & Lambert, 1978a, 1978b).

The PELCO.

The PELCO, introduced in 1977 as the Projet d'Enseignement des Langues d'origine [PELO], involves the teaching of heritage languages within the regular school system for approximately 100 hours per year. The classes are generally offered for 30 minutes per day, usually outside the regular school day, but in some cases within the school's daily timetable. The Ministry of Education covers the cost of teachers' salaries and teaching materials and has also developed the curriculum and teachers' guides for each of the languages offered. The Ministry also helps provide periodic professional development workshops to assist teachers in implementing the program. Although for a time the PELO was offered only in French language schools, it has been available in both English and French educational sectors since 1982. In 1986/87 there were 12 languages taught to 4,924 students in PELCO (Canadian Ethnocultural Council, 1988).

Not surprisingly in the wake of the controversy surrounding Bill 101, the ethnic communities initially tended to be suspicious of the Quebec government's motives behind the program, and many regular teachers and principals also reacted negatively. Some ethnic community leaders denounced the program as a political ploy to attract the ethnic vote and argued that it would take community control over the transmission of language and culture away from the ethnic groups themselves. Ethnic parents were concerned that their children might fall behind in academic subject matter which had been replaced by the heritage language classes in the regular school day. Community leaders who welcomed the program pointed out that some of those who reacted negatively had a conflict of interest in that they were involved in teaching heritage languages in community-run supplementary schools.

At a political level, the PELCO clearly forms part of a strategy to integrate ethnocultural communities into a francophone Quebec society but it attempts to achieve this goal in a way that is consistent with the stated principles of interculturalism rather than through forced assimilation. The stated societal aim of the PELCO is to encourage mutual respect among adjoining cultures and to achieve harmony in diversity (Bureau des Services aux Communautés Culturelles, 1983, p. 4).

Several advantages of the PELCO over programs that are operated by the ethnocultural communities themselves are noted in government documents. For example, it is suggested that the quality of teaching is improved as a result of the pedagogical support offered by the Ministry and school boards; the courses are recognised for credit by the Ministry of Education; the objectives and content are inspired by the Quebec environment and integrated with the content of the regular school curriculum; there is significant participation by members of the ethnocultural communities in program development and, of course, teaching. All of these factors, it is suggested, enhance children's appreciation of their own culture.

Community-Operated Supplementary Schools.

The Programme des Langues Ethniques (PLE) has been in existence since 1970 and consists of financial support administered through the Ministry of Cultural Communities and Immigration for the teaching of heritage languages by the ethnic communities themselves outside the regular public school system (usually on Saturday mornings or after regular school hours). Grant subsidies are primarily directed towards the cost of renting approved classroom space from boards of education.

Recipients of subsidies must be members of the Council of Ethnic Language Classes, be incorporated under Quebec law and be in possession of a permit under the Private Education Act. The Council of Ethnic Language Classes acts as an advisory body to the Ministry with regard to heritage language education. More than 19,000 students from 35 language groups are involved in these classes (Canadian Ethnocultural Council, 1988).

The contribution of the Quebec government through the PLE represents about 10% of the total operating costs of the schools. A similar proportion is supplied by the federal government through its Cultural Enrichment Program while support is also provided by certain countries of origin. The ethnocultural communities themselves support about 76% of the operating costs, almost half of this percentage being supplied through fees charged to parents (Comité d'Implantation du Plan d'Action a l'Intention des Communautés Culturelles, 1983, p. 36). Thus, unlike the PELCO, programs supported by the Programme des Langues Ethniques operate on a fee-paying basis and thus may exclude students whose families are recent arrivals or who lack the financial means to pay for heritage language teaching.

High school students who are registered in community-run programs approved by the Ministry of Education can receive credit for these courses. As of 1986, eleven language and culture programs had been approved: Greek, Polish, German, Armenian, Swahili, Spanish, Korean, Chinese, Italian, Yiddish and Jewish culture (Canadian Ethnocultural Council, 1988).

In summary, the numbers of students served under the PELCO and PLE have increased steadily during the past decade. Although initially controversial, the PELO/PELCO has been largely accepted by ethnocultural communities. Tensions surrounding the maintenance of heritage languages and cultures are likely to grow in Quebec as immigration increases and the French school systems become even more culturally and linguistically diverse.

Heritage Language Programs in Ontario

In response to the federal multiculturalism policy, the Ontario provincial government and some of the larger school boards set up Task Forces and Work Groups in the early seventies to formulate policies and programs with respect to the cultural diversity in their respective jurisdictions. The extent of the reorientation implied by the recognition of multiculturalism was expressed in the Toronto Board of Education's Work Group Draft Report on Multiculturalism published in 1975:

> The shocking recognition for the Board of Education for the City of Toronto is that within the space of a decade its CULTUR-AL BASE HAS BECOME INCOMPATIBLE (emphasis original) with the cultural base of the society which supports its endeavour (p. 5).

The policies and programs that have been developed to realign the cultural base of school programs with those of communities at both provincial and local school board levels have focused on issues such as textbook bias, multicultural materials development, race relations, school-community relations, and training of teachers and other school personnel. For the most part, these issues have not aroused the passions of the general public to any great extent and the directions proposed by the Toronto Board and by other Boards of Education with respect to these issues have been applauded by the media.·

The reaction of the public and of the media to heritage language teaching, however, has, as I've indicated, been very different. The debate on heritage language provision has gone through five distinct phases since the early 1970's, each phase representing a slight but highly contested erosion of Anglo-conformity in both public policy and public attitude.

Phase I. Initial Skirmishes

The first shot in what subsequently turned into Toronto's heritage language battle was fired in April 1972; it was a proposal made by Anthony Grande, a teacher in the Toronto Board, for an Italian-English bilingual program (see Lind, 1974; Grande, 1975). According to Lind "when Grande first made his proposal in April, the New Canadian Committee [of the Toronto Board] went apoplectic" (p. 48-49). The Board heard a modified version of the plan one year later and after considerable negotiation with the Ministry of Education about what was permissible under the Schools Administration Act, a kindergarten Italian transition program emerged. At the same time the Board approved "bicultural/bilingual immersion" programs for Chinese and Greek students. The term "immersion" is clearly a misnomer since all that was involved was 30 minutes a day of instruction in Chinese or Greek culture (and some language) taught by volunteers. In the case of Chinese, the program was on a withdrawal basis during the school day in two schools, while the Greek program was taught after regular school hours (see Desosaran and Gershman, 1976, for an evaluation of the Chinese program).

Lind (1974) describes the Ministry of Education during these debates as "without clear policy, except to unbend as little as necessary to avoid confrontation" (p. 50).

Phase II. The Work Group on Multicultural Programs

In May 1974 the Toronto Board set up the Work Group on Multicultural Programs to investigate philosophy and programs related to the city's multicultural population. The Work Group published a Draft Report in 1975 and a Final Report in the following year.

The Draft Report recommended the the Board request the Ministry of Education to amend the Ontario Education Act to allow languages other than English and French to be used both as languages and subjects of instruction at the elementary level (Toronto Board of Education, 1975). The Report also recommended that existing "bicultural-bilingual" and transition programs be continued and expanded and that the Board continue to be responsive to requests for the institution of third language subject credit courses at the secondary school level.

These recommendations were based on the strong ethnocultural community support in the briefs and consultations for proposals related to the promotion of original culture and language (see Masemann, 1978/79). However, the Work Group's Final Report rescinded what were perceived as the more radical of their recommendations in the face of outrage from certain sectors of the community. They point out that publication of the Draft Report evoked a response from "newly participating groups in opposition to certain 'ideas' contained in the report" (1976, p. 23-24). Concerns with ghettoization and cost were mixed with charges that "ethnic demands" were outrageous; specifically, it was felt by many that immigrants or their parents or grandparents chose to come to Canada. They should therefore accept the existing educational and social system. If they chose to maintain their home language it should be done "quietly" in the home. The view was also strongly expressed that language maintenance, whether in the home or school, was educationally ill-advised because it would impede students' acquisition of English.

The strength of this "significant minority opinion" together with the Ministry's refusal to change the Education Act led the Work Group to withdraw its recommendations relating to third language teaching.

Phase III. The Heritage Languages Program (HLP)

The HLP was announced in the spring of 1977 and represented a carefully considered attempt to accommodate the persistent "ethnic demands" while minimizing the backlash from those opposed to publicly supported heritage language teaching. An influential factor in the government's decision to institute the program was the fact that the Metropolitan Separate School Board (MSSB) had been offering an Italian language and culture program within its schools for several years that was funded by the Italian government (Berryman, 1986; Danesi and DiGiovanni, 1989). In 1975/76, for example, the Italian Government provided $187,000 to the MSSB for the Italian language and culture program (Berryman, 1986). Berryman points out that

> This apparent interference by a foreign government in the Ontario schooling process, which, undoubtedly was a definite concern of the Government of Ontario, had a strong impact on the Government to finally adopt its Heritage Languages Program (1986, p. 37).

While this "interference" was irksome to the Ontario government, they were powerless to stop it. Both the MSSB and the numerically very significant Italian community in Toronto were naturally unwilling to refuse the funding in the absence of any commitment from the Ontario government to support language maintenance efforts.

The prospect that other foreign governments might also get involved and the increasing demographic significance of ethnocultural communities led to what was essentially a political decision to institute the HLP. The timing of the announcement was suspiciously close to a provincial election in which the government was hoping to attract the ethnic vote in Metropolitan Toronto.

In chronicling these developments, Berryman (1986) points out that a competitive climate had arisen between the MSSB and the public boards as a result of the transfer of numerous students of mainly Italian origin to the separate board in the early 1970s:

This situation motivated all school boards to become more sensitive to the needs and wishes of their multiethnic and multilinguistic populations. For the public school systems, it was inevitable: either provide quality multicultural programs or lose more pupils. ... As the Government of Ontario monitored these events, especially the infusion of monies into Ontario schools by a foreign government to finance its program for Ontario students that was not fully controlled by an Ontario schools board, pressures to make changes to the Education Act became too onerous to ignore. It was inevitable, therefore, that approval for the study of non-official languages in Ontario's elementary schools would soon occur (1986, p. 54-55).

There are three basic options for when classes may be held under the HLP: (a) on weekends; (b) after the regular 5-hour school day; and (3) integrated into a school day extended by half-an-hour. This last option continues to be the predominant one in the MSSB which operates by far the largest program (more than 30,000 students enrolled).

Because the HLP is funded under the Continuing Education Program, instructors need not have Ontario teaching certification and can be paid at a considerably lower rate than regular certified teachers. Also, no major changes were required in the provincial Education Act since the program was being offered outside regular school hours. Thus, for the Ontario government, the HLP appeared to represent a reasonable compromise whereby the concerns of ethnic communities could be accommodated without excessively alienating other community interests. However, the initial reaction of those opposed to the program was vehemently hostile. In the words of a Ministry official, the phone rang constantly for three weeks with people voicing their disapproval.

The Ministry also appears to have been caught off-guard by the demand for the program. Costs for 1977/78 had been estimated at $1-1.5 million but actually totalled about 5 million and continued to rise for several subsequent years as enrolment increased to a plateau of slightly above 90,000 students. During the initial 1977/78 school year, 42 school boards provided 2,000 classes in 30 different languages to more than 50,000 students. Nine years later in 1986/87 the numbers had increased to 72 school boards offering 4,364 classes in 58 different languages to 91,110 students at a cost of $11.5 million (Canadian Ethnocultural Council, 1988). In addition, more than 69,000 students are enrolled in 369 heritage language schools operated by ethnocultural community groups that receive funding from the federal government's Cultural Enrichment Program. There is some overlap between these figures as some students are enrolled both in the provincial HLP and in supplementary school programs. While no fees are involved for the program funded by the Ontario government (to a limit of two-and-one-half hours per week), the major costs for additional class time operated by community groups are borne by the parents on a fee-paying basis.

In the year after the program was introduced an attempt was made by the Ministry of Education to change the formula under which the HLP was funded. This would have substantially cut the funds available for the program from Ministry sources. However, determined opposition from ethnocultural community groups convinced the government that it was not politically feasible to take away something that had already been given and the proposal was withdrawn. The remainder of the Conservative government's term was marked by inaction on the HLP on the grounds that it was a "no-win" situation politically. No attempt was made to consolidate the program nor to increase the effectiveness of program delivery but neither was any further attempt made to cut it back.

In assessing the impact of the Heritage Languages policy initiative, Berryman (1986) concludes that:

> ...it was, in effect, a victory for ethnocultural community leaders and their members who finally placed one foot inside the door of the educational establishment. The principle that language and culture are inseparably connected was at least being partially recognised. (p. 62)

For the Ministry, however, the experience of implementing the HLP brought home the cost, both financial and political, of accommodating any further to "ethnic demands."

Phase IV. The Third Language Workgroup Report (1982)

As a result of dissatisfaction with aspects of the HLP, most notably its implication that heritage language teaching was not a legitimate part of students' "regular" education, the Ukrainian and Armenian communities placed proposals before the Toronto Board in the spring of 1980 for the establishment of "Alternative Language Schools," essentially magnet schools in which the heritage language would be taught for half-an-hour during an extended school day but school announcements and incidental "non-instructional" conversation could also be in the heritage language as a means of providing students with a greater amount of meaningful input in the language. These proposals evoked a public outcry of "ghettoization" and "balkanization" and were savaged by the press.

In June 1980, the Toronto Board referred the entire question of third language instruction to a Work Group. After extensive community consultation and visits to the Ukrainian-English programs in western Canada, the Work Group issued its final report in March 1982. It recommended that the heritage language program should be gradually integrated into a regular extended school day where feasible and also that, as a long-term strategy, the board work towards the implementation of bilingual and trilingual programs involving heritage languages and pressure the Ministry to enact the necessary enabling legislation.

The ensuing debate was divisive and bitter. A large proportion of the ethnocultural communities strongly supported the Work Group proposals while much of the opposition came from the Anglo-Canadian community. However, some individuals from ethnocultural community backgrounds also vocally opposed the proposals. Teachers' Federations were also strongly opposed to the proposals on the grounds that the school system was already overloaded. Almost 200 oral submissions were made to the board during three marathon sessions that lasted into the early hours of the morning. Supporters of the opposing sides loudly voiced their approval or disapproval of each submission, and there were frequent verbal confrontations in the corridors of the board offices. Despite the controversy, on May 5 1982 the board, dominated by trustees aligned with the New Democratic Party (NDP), approved the Report and in 1983-84 the process of integrating the HLP into about a dozen Toronto schools began.

The controversy did not end there, however. Any school "targeted" for integration had to carry out a community vote on the issue and these debates within communities were often divisive. For the most part, teachers were strongly opposed to integration and in some cases their views on the issue were communicated either directly or indirectly to students. For example, some parents reported that teachers had told their children that their grades would suffer if the program were integrated into the school.

The Toronto Teachers' Federation (TTF) submitted the matter for arbitration and organized a "work-to-rule" by the teachers in which all extra-curricular activities were boycotted. A full-scale strike was also threatened on the issue. The teachers' concerns were expressed by the President of the TTF as follows:

> Regardless of one's opinions about the merits of the 'integrated' school day, what is abundantly clear is that the price has been too high. Stress in the workplace, low morale, inequities in hours of work, adverse effects on core program, remedial help and extra-curricular activities are more than mere irritants. (McFadyen, 1983, p.2)

Although the arbitration report supported the board's right to implement the integrated/extended school day, by that time (Autumn 1985) new school board elections had altered the balance of power on the board. The NDP-aligned trustees were now in a minority and the conservative majority were firmly opposed to the integration of the heritage language program. The new board took no immediate action against the integrated heritage language program, but they did disband the School-Community Relations Department (SCR) which had been active in providing information to parents from ethnocultural communities about heritage language issues and encouraging them to attend meetings in which the issues were being discussed. The coordinator of the SCR was relieved of his duties "because of the unavailability of work" (*Role Call*, Volume 9, no. 1, November 1986, p. 8).

The basic arguments in the debate were not very different from those in previous Toronto debates on the issue, although the pitch and level of community involvement were undoubtedly more shrill. Those arguing for the Work Group Report stressed the pain of language and culture loss among their children and invoked the research findings summarized in the Report that supported both heritage language teaching in general and bilingual and trilingual programs in particular. The validity of bilingualism and trilingualism as educational goals for their children was stressed.

Opponents tended to focus on the presumed financial and social consequences of implementing the Report. A letter to the *Globe and Mail* on April 17 1982 by Trustee Michael Walker painted a grim picture of these probable consequences:

> If this report is passed, it would probably result in the segregation of children along linguistic and cultural lines, the busing of children on a major scale across the city, using linguistic and cultural quota to staff schools with teachers and very large additional costs to the taxpayer The recommendations of this report will guarantee second-class status to any student attending a third language school and be of great disservice to the community at large. I also believe it will ultimately tear the public school system apart in Toronto.

It is clear that this debate escalated beyond the merits or otherwise of the specific proposals contained in the Work Group Report. The concerns of opponents were not diminished by the presence of almost 30,000 students in integrated heritage language classes in the MSSB at no extra cost to the taxpayer and no evidence of ghettoization nor academic difficulties as a result of the program (Keyser and Brown, 1980).

An indication of where the general public throughout Ontario stood on the issue is given in the fourth OISE survey on public attitudes toward education (Livingstone and Hart, 1983). More than one third of all respondents felt that no provision should be made for teaching heritage languages in elementary schools while about the same number thought that provision should be made after school where there was sufficient interest. Considerably fewer respondents favoured teaching heritage languages during the school day either as a subject (24%) or a medium of instruction (6%). Respondents with lower income and educational levels tended to be more opposed to heritage language provision than those with higher levels of income and education.

Phase V. Consolidation of the HLP

When the Liberal Party was elected to power in Ontario in the mid-eighties, it proclaimed that issues related to multiculturalism and race relations were a priority. Informal consultations were begun with respect to policy initiatives that should be undertaken to consolidate the HLP. Since its inception, emotions surrounding the program had simmered close to boiling point, but little effort had been made by the Ministry of Education to validate and strengthen its educational status. Apart from a literature review on the issue (Cummins, 1983), no research had been funded on the effects of the program and minimal funds had been made available for curriculum development and teacher in-service.

The Ministry published a discussion document on June 8, 1987, entitled *Proposal for Action: Ontario's Heritage Languages Program* which proposed several initiatives to consolidate the program. Implementation of the program by a school board would be required if 25 or more parents with children in the board requested it, and support would be provided for curriculum development, dissemination of resources, teacher training, and research. The Ministry did not propose to change the Education Act to permit heritage languages to be used as languages of instruction within the school day. The proposal to make implementation of the program mandatory for school boards was primarily directed against the Scarborough Board of Education that had steadfastly refused to implement the program despite strong pressure from ethnocultural communities.

The public was invited to respond to these proposals and these responses were compiled by the Ministry (Davis, 1987). The proposal to make the program mandatory elicited the most reaction with the usual arguments for and against heritage languages being advanced; it was suggested, for example, that the education system has many more pressing problems to resolve (e.g. the high rate of illiteracy among young people, school drop-out, curriculum overload, etc) and that teaching heritage languages will diminish students' acquisition of English and French. Heritage language teaching was also seen as socially divisive and boards of education were concerned about the reduction of school board autonomy. On the opposite side, it was argued that heritage language programs will contribute to the development of global citizens and lessen the potential for intra-familial conflict by removing the cultural barrier between children and adults. The economic value of proficiency in heritage languages was also advanced as an argument in favour of strengthening the program.

In the absence of serious opposition, the Ministry went ahead and in 1988/89 began to implement the proposals it had put forward. *A Curriculum Guideline for Heritage Languages* was developed during 1989 and the Scarborough Board reluctantly joined the program in September 1989.

Politically, the Ministry has succeeded in consolidating and, to some extent, legitimizing the HLP without risking the political upheaval that would likely have ensued if enabling legislation had been passed to permit heritage languages to be used as languages of instruction. The lack of widespread ethnocultural community pressure for using heritage languages for instructional purposes undoubtedly reinforces, in the Ministry's view, the political wisdom of omitting this initiative from its *Proposal for Action*.[3] However, from an educational perspective, the recent initiatives do little to alter the marginal status of heritage language teaching and they continue to impose constraints on school boards and communities that might wish to respond in a more imaginative and effective way to the linguistic diversity of the school population.

Heritage Language Teaching in the Prairie Provinces

Three major types of provision for heritage language instruction can be distinguished in the Prairie provinces: first, bilingual programs within the regular public school system involving the use of a heritage language as a medium of instruction for about 50% of the school day; second, programs funded by provincial governments and administered by local school boards in which the heritage language is taught as a core subject within the regular school day; third, part-time programs operated on weekends or after school hours by the ethnocultural communities themselves, usually with federal and provincial government financial support.

Bilingual Heritage Language Programs.

In 1971 Alberta became the first province to legalize languages other than English or French as mediums of instruction in the public school system, largely as a result of pressure from the Ukrainian community. Saskatchewan followed in 1978 and Manitoba in 1979. Currently, Ukrainian and German bilingual programs involving up to 100% instruction through the heritage language in kindergarten and up to 50% thereafter are in operation in all three provinces and are financially supported by provincial governments.[4] Hebrew bilingual programs also exist in Alberta and Manitoba and a Yiddish-English bilingual program is also available in Edmonton. Bilingual English-Chinese and English-Arabic programs were established in September 1983 in the Edmonton Public School Board and a Polish-English program operates in the Edmonton Catholic Schools. It is interesting to note that the Chinese program offers instruction in Mandarin although most of the children in the program come from Cantonese home backgrounds. The parents are conscious of the higher status and utility of Mandarin and thus the program is very much an immersion program for these children (Jones, 1984). In the 1986/87 school year, the total enrolment in Alberta's bilingual programs was 2,800 (Canadian Ethnocultural Council, 1988).

The Ukrainian programs have been evaluated in both Alberta and Manitoba with very positive results. Essentially, children acquire considerable proficiency in the heritage language at no cost to their development of English or other academic skills (Edmonton Public Schools, 1980; Chapman, 1981; Ewanyshyn, 1980). Thus, the findings are analogous to those of French immersion and minority Francophone program evaluations (see Cummins, 1983 for a review). An important difference, however, is that the socio-economic profile of students in the Ukrainian program is similar to that of the school board at large whereas French immersion programs have typically catered to a higher socio-economic group. Thus, the Ukrainian program evaluations suggest that bilingual education is not just for an elite group of students but is appropriate for a large proportion of the school population.

The major problem that exists for these programs relates to

their relatively low enrolments (as a result of the fact that the participating ethnocultural groups often tend not to be concentrated in particular urban and rural areas) and the unwillingness of some school boards to assume responsibility for operating the program. However, these enrichment bilingual programs are unique in North America and demonstrate the educational feasibility of such an approach.

These programs have also had considerable impact on the heritage language debates elsewhere in Canada. For example, they were highlighted in the Toronto Board's Work Group Report on Third Languages (1982) and Shaw (1983) suggests that a similar approach is appropriate to revive the fortunes of Gaelic in Cape Breton:

> Within Canada, the successful English-Ukrainian bilingual programs in areas of Manitoba and Alberta have provided a most encouraging and instructive example which should be followed in Cape Breton. (1983, p. 75)

The fact that the demand for these programs among ethnocultural groups in the Prairie provinces is relatively modest suggests that the fears of some Ontario policy-makers that school boards would be swamped by demand for bilingual programs if the Ontario legislation were changed are groundless. They represent an alternative approach to the development and maintenance of language skills that is unlikely to appeal to more than a handful of ethnocultural communities.

Heritage Languages as Subjects of Instruction within the Public School.

In the Prairie provinces a limited number of modern languages other than French and English have been offered at the secondary level as optional subjects. For example, in Saskatchewan, a second language requirement was introduced in 1967 for grades 7-9 students and German and Ukrainian curriculum committees were established in the following year in order to develop programs in these languages. In Manitoba, secondary programs in heritage languages have existed since the 1950's and elementary programs that teach the language within the regular school day were introduced in the seventies.

In the 1986/87 school year, nine core second languages were

offered in Manitoba, two in Saskatchewan (Ukrainian and German) and six in Alberta. For the most part, these languages are offered at both elementary and secondary levels.

Programs Operated by Ethnocultural Communities.

More than 10,000 students in both Alberta and Manitoba are enrolled in supplementary schools supported by the federal government while more than 2,000 students in Saskatchewan are enrolled in such programs. In addition, the provincial governments in all three provinces provide financial support for the teaching of heritage languages in supplementary schools. Manitoba has a total of close to 30,000 students studying heritage languages in out-of-school situations.

All three Prairie provinces have very active heritage language associations that organize in-service sessions for teachers and consult regularly with the provincial governments with respect to policy and programs to support heritage language teaching. This contrasts with the situation in Ontario where the functioning of the Ontario Heritage Language Association has been sporadic.

Recent policy documents in the Prairie provinces reinforce the importance of heritage language instruction, although government enthusiasm often appears to be considerably weaker than that of ethnocultural communities. For example, the *Language Education Policy for Alberta (1988)* states

> Alberta Education supports the provision of opportunities for students who wish to acquire or maintain languages other than English or French so that they may have access to a partial immersion (bilingual) program or second language courses in languages other than English or French. *(Government of Alberta, 1988, p. 16)*[5]

Similarly, a recent report on *Multiculturalism in Saskatchewan* recommended that the Department of Education assume responsibility for both in-school and out-of-school heritage language instruction in the province and make "well-supported heritage language instruction a priority in Saskatchewan" (1989, p. 21). In addition, it was recommended that the universities establish programs to train and certify heritage language teachers. These recommendations closely reflect the submission made by the Saskatchewan Organization for Heritage Languages (SOHL) to the committee. The SOHL brief emphasized that "It is time that the Government of Saskatchewan recognize that heritage languages are Canadian languages and their value to Canadian society and the economy has been vastly underestimated" (*SOHL Newsletter*, Winter, 1988, p. 1).

Saskatchewan Education recently (March 1989) announced interim directions for heritage language policy in the province in response to an advisory committee on heritage languages that had submitted its report three years previously. Among the initiatives that are envisaged are establishing a mechanism to give students credit standing for proficiency gained in heritage languages studied after school and creation of a special heritage language teaching certificate (see *TEMA*, Summer 1989, Vol. 20, No. 2).

In short, a much closer relationship exists between government agencies and community-based heritage language organizations in the Prairie provinces than is the case in most other parts of Canada. Although, from the perspective of SOHL, the Saskatchewan government has been slow to respond to recommendations for upgrading the provision of heritage language instruction, the climate in the Prairie provinces is generally favourable towards heritage languages, and the issues are not nearly so contentious as in Ontario and Quebec. Clearly, this favourable climate is partly due to the demographic make-up of the Prairie provinces with their large well-established Ukrainian and German populations. The left-wing/right-wing split that, with some exceptions, is apparent in the Ontario context is not nearly so evident in the prairie provinces. For example, during the late seventies and early eighties, conservative governments in Alberta and NDP governments in Manitoba appear to have responded to ethnocultural community aspirations with equal vigour.

Heritage Language Provision in British Columbia.

During the 1986/87 school year, 14,590 students were enrolled in 140 supplementary schools that received financial support from the federal government. Twenty-six languages were taught in these schools. The provincial government does not provide funds directly for heritage language instruction although its recent Pacific Rim initiative encourages the establishment of innovative programs in economically-significant Pacific Rim languages within the regular school system. Although no major provincial funding is provided for heritage language instruction, the Education Act in British Columbia does not prevent school districts from offering bilingual or core subject heritage language programs, as is the case in Ontario. The Ministry of Education also offers credit to students who are taking approved heritage language courses at the secondary level either in community-run or regular school programs.

One Russian-English bilingual program was started in 1983 and continues to operate in school district No. 9 at Castlegar. Hebrew-English bilingual programs operate in some independent schools in the Vancouver area.

Heritage Languages in the Atlantic Provinces.

As of 1986/87 approximately 1,500 students were enrolled in supplementary language programs that received funds from the federal government. No financial assistance is provided by the provincial governments of the area, and no classes are taught within the regular school program. Arabic is the most commonly taught heritage language in the Atlantic provinces.

One recent development in the Atlantic provinces that is potentially of major significance for heritage language teaching elsewhere in Canada is the establishment of a Gaelic language playgroup in the Iona district of Cape Breton. *Croileagan a'Chaolais* is modelled after very successful Gaelic playgroups in Scotland and Ireland and aims to surround the child with the sounds of Gaelic from a very early age. Rosemary MacCormack, the playgroup leader, writing about the program in the Autumn 1989 issue of *Forerunner*, a Cape Breton Community Magazine, notes that "already most of the youngsters who have attended regularly since the program started in December 1988 can understand what is being said to them in Gaelic and can repeat phrases and the words of two or three songs" (MacCormack, 1989, p. 12). However, the program is staffed only by volunteers and problems of continued funding are not fully resolved.

Conclusion

During the past decade there has been a rapid expansion of heritage language teaching provision in most parts of Canada. Both federal and provincial funds have contributed to this expansion. However, as foreshadowed by the *Majority Attitudes Study* in 1977, public opinion is divided on the merits of government support for heritage language teaching, particularly within the regular school system. The issue has been most divisive in Ontario where teachers in the Toronto Board of Education worked to rule for a six month period in order to protest against the school board's plans to integrate the program within an extended school day. In Quebec, the combination of increased immigration and the fact that children from ethnocultural backgrounds must attend schools in the French sector has resulted in increased tensions surrounding issues of language and culture. The continuing low birthrate in Quebec suggests that these issues will likely continue to be controversial as the province becomes increasingly diverse culturally and linguistically. By contrast, the issue has been largely non-contentious in the Prairie provinces where full bilingual programs are in operation for the teaching of a number of languages.

The "persistent ambiguities" regarding the relation between multiculturalism and multilingualism that early commentators noted in the multiculturalism policy, while still in evidence, have begun to yield to cautious endorsement of multilingualism as a valid societal goal. The pace of change is gradual, but there has been definite consolidation of heritage language provision at both federal and provincial levels of government. The inevitability of increased immigration to Canada to compensate for the falling birthrate means that linguistic diversity will undoubtedly expand and the dominance of Anglo-Canadian perspectives is likely to continue to decline. However, during this period of rapid change in the demographics of Canadian society, tensions surrounding the relative balance of power between "us" and "them" are likely to escalate, as happened repeatedly in the Toronto Board of Education during the past decade.

In the past, the dominant Anglo-Celtic group provided two major options to ethnocultural communities with respect to language and culture: either give up their languages and cultures and become invisible and inaudible through assimilation or, alternatively, maintain their languages and cultures but do it "quietly," at their own expense without in any way affecting the linguistic and cultural status quo or the political power structure. The increasing demographic strength and economic security of many ethnocultural communities have allowed them to reject these two options and articulate their priorities as Canadian taxpayers. What is being challenged by ethnocultural communities outside Quebec is the core value of Anglo-conformity that persists beneath the veneer of multiculturalism among a significant proportion of the Canadian public.

Within Quebec, the impetus for Franco-conformity is a more recent phenomenon with very different roots than Anglo-conformity in the rest of Canada. In fact, strong nationalist sentiment expressed in terms of Quebec separatism dates from about the time when "multiculturalism" became official federal government policy in the early seventies, although its roots obviously go back further. Quebec government policy is relatively coherent in its emphasis on interculturalism within a francophone milieu together with financial support for heritage language maintenance; however, as acknowledged in government documents, many Québécois find it difficult to accept the reality of racial, cultural and linguistic diversity even within the context of a society where the primacy of both the French language and common Quebec culture is no longer seriously contested by the majority of ethnocultural communities. Ethnocultural communities in Quebec enjoy a broader range of options for language maintenance and development than is the case in Ontario as a result of the generous funding of private schools that are permitted to use a heritage language as a partial medium of instruction as well as provincial government support for both community-operated heritage language programs and the teaching of heritage languages in public schools. The major struggle for ethnocultural groups in Quebec during the next 20 years is likely to focus on breaking down the barriers to full and equal participation in all spheres of Quebec life as the francophone majority adapts to the reality of cultural and racial diversity. This is clearly also a priority for ethnocultural groups outside of Quebec, but issues of financial and legislative support for heritage language maintenance are likely to be equally prominent.

In short, while a superficial notion of multiculturalism has come to be associated with Canadian identity (at least outside of Quebec) as a value that sets us apart from our American neighbours, a more grounded notion of multiculturalism involving equal access to power and resources for all cultural groups has yet to take root in the Canadian psyche.

In view of the conflict that has characterized the Canadian debate on heritage languages, it is essential to examine critically the rationale for promoting children's maintenance and acquisition of these languages. As we have seen, it is difficult to disentangle the political and educational issues as a result of the fact that the debate is so emotionally charged. Thus, in the next chapter we attempt to summarize the educational and social rationale for promoting heritage languages in the Canadian context.

FOOTNOTES

[1] The Institute will receive $500,000 each year for 5 years for operating expenses and $800,000 each year for 5 years to be placed into an endowment to secure long-term financing.

[2] There are a considerable number of programs for teaching Native and Inuit languages in the Northwest Territories and the Yukon but consideration of these programs is outside the scope of the present volume.

[3] There is still pressure for change to the Education Act from some ethnocultural communities. For example, an editorial in the December-January (1988/89) issue of *New Perspectives* (a Ukrainian community newspaper) notes that the Supreme Court of Canada ruled in December 1988 that "Language is not merely a means or medium of expression; it colors the content and meaning of expression. It is a means by which a people may express

its cultural identity. ... Language is so intimately related to the form and content of expression that there cannot be true freedom of expression if one is prevented from using the language of one's choice." The editorial argues that the denial of the possibility of Ukrainian-English bilingual education in Ontario is in violation of the Supreme Court's interpretation of the Charter of Rights and Freedoms with respect to language and calls on the Ukrainian community to test the issue in the courts (see also Wynnyckyj, 1989a).

[4] For reviews of the political pressures brought to bear in the early 1970s by the Ukrainian community in effecting a change in provincial legislation and establishing the initial Ukrainian-English bilingual programs see Lupul (1976) and Mallea (1989).

[5] Although the continuation of bilingual heritage language programs are guaranteed in the policy, some ethnocultural communities in Alberta, particularly the Ukrainian community, are concerned that the policy does not more strongly promote the spread of these programs (Wynnyckyj, 1989b). There is concern that the government regards them as worthy only of benign neglect with the assumption that they will die a natural death as their novelty evaporates and enrolments dwindle.

Chapter 4

Language as Human Resource
The Rationale and Research Support for Heritage Language Promotion

Two broad categories of heritage or minority language provision can be distinguished in programs throughout the world. The first category involves the transitional use of the minority language as a temporary bridge to help children keep up with academic content while they are acquiring proficiency in the school language. Such transitional bilingual programs are common in the United States and have also been implemented in some European countries. The major goal is to promote educational equity for minority children rather than development of heritage language skills. In other words, despite the fact that the programs are bilingual (at least temporarily), the linguistic goals encompass only monolingualism. By contrast, enrichment heritage language programs use the minority language as a medium of instruction or teach the language as a subject on a longer-term basis in order to develop proficiency in that language as well as in the majority language. The goal is bilingualism or trilingualism. Whereas transitional programs are usually intended only for students from minority language backgrounds, enrichment programs may involve students from both minority and majority backgrounds.

Some transitional heritage language programs were implemented in Canada during the 1970's but the vast majority of programs are of the enrichment type (see Appendix for documentation on Canadian bilingual and heritage language teaching programs). Their primary goal is to promote students' proficiency in the heritage language. The goals of these programs have been made explicit in a number of documents produced by provincial governments and heritage language organizations. For example, the Saskatchewan Organization for Heritage Languages (SOHL) has published a brochure outlining the rationale for studying heritage languages; among the reasons given for learning heritage languages are that learning other languages fosters:

◆ Deeper appreciation of human intelligence and the human capacity for speech;

◆ Enhanced intellectual development;

◆ Greater understanding and appreciation of one's cultural roots;

◆ Greater understanding and appreciation of one's first language;

◆ Better communication within family, community, nation and the world.[1]

Similarly, the rationale for the Ontario Heritage Languages Program expressed by the Ministry of Education clearly emphasizes the enrichment potential of heritage language promotion. According to the information pamphlet on the program (Ministry of Education, no date), the opportunity to develop heritage language reading, writing and speaking skills will:

◆ Enhance the students' concept of themselves and their heritage;

◆ Improve communication with parents and grandparents;

◆ Prepare students to use heritage languages in the Canadian context;

◆ Allow students to use skills and concepts they already possess;

◆ Provide experiences in learning that may prove a valuable basis for credit courses at the high school level;

◆ Encourage all students to develop new language skills that will help them to function more effectively in Canada's multicultural environment as well as in the international community.

A survey carried out by the Toronto Board of Education (Larter & Cheng, 1986) showed that 88 percent of respondents (569 out of 644) who included principals, teachers, heritage language instructors, and parents of children in integrated/extended day schools felt that children should learn their heritage language for the following major reasons:

◆ To improve communications with relatives;

◆ To enhance pride in heritage;

◆ To maintain and revitalize culture and religion; and

◆ Because languages are best learned when young.

Programs of minority language promotion in other parts of the world have tended to place more explicit emphasis on the role of language maintenance and development in alleviating the academic problems that many minority students are reported to experience (see Cummins 1983 for a review). Bilingual programs for minority students are now widespread in the United States, and in Europe the European Community has issued a directive strongly encouraging member states to take steps to teach the mother tongue and culture of the country of origin of minority students. The rationale underlying this directive is made explicit in a European Commission document:

> No one now disputes that the successful integration of immigrants into the host countries' schools requires special education measures. The great innovation of recent years is that the mother tongue is now regarded as a significant component of the child's personality, which is crucial to his psychological wellbeing and facilitates integration into a new environment. *(European Commission, 1978, p. 15).*

Although the provisions take various forms and are often controversial (see Skutnabb-Kangas and Cummins, 1988), an increasing number of western industrialized countries have endorsed some form of mother tongue support for minority students. The research basis for promoting children's competence in their mother tongue is also international in scope. The tence in their mother tongue is also international in scope. The rationale for such provision is well summarized by Catherine Snow and Kenji Hakuta (1989), two of the most international-ly-prominent researchers in this area. Snow and Hakuta suggest that in the American context the appropriate issue to focus on is not the costs of heritage language promotion but the costs of monolingualism:

> ...the rapid shift into English means that children who could have learned fluent Spanish or Chinese or Portuguese from their mothers and grandmothers are instead struggling to learn it, and often succeeding poorly, in high school foreign language classes. Aside from the communication gap that is created across generations of immigrants by this shift, there are many other costs associated with the melting pot's shift into monolingual English.

> Costs to society includes:

> Educational costs: We need to devote teachers, schooltime, and part of the educational budget to foreign language training ... and the resultant levels of fluency and correctness of foreign language students are much lower than those of children who have learned these languages at home.

> Economic competitiveness: American multinational businesses and foreign service and intelligence operations are severely hampered by the low numbers of Americans competent in languages other than English.

> National security costs: Millions of dollars are spent annually training foreign service personnel, military personnel, and spies in foreign languages.

> Costs to the individual include:

> Time and effort: It takes time, effort, commitment, motivation and hard work to learn a foreign language in high school, and much less effort just to maintain a language already learned at home.

> Cognitive cost: there is some evidence suggesting that monolingual children are missing out on an opportunity to develop an early appreciation of language that results in better ability to perform well on tasks requiring linguistic and cognitive flexibility. (1989, p. 2-3)

In our view, far more significant for Canadian (and American) society than either lack of economic competitiveness or paranoia about "national security" are the costs of monolingualism with respect to Canada's ability to cooperate in a non-condescending way with other countries in searching for solutions to increasingly urgent global environmental and social problems. Nonetheless, the narrowly-conceived economic and diplomatic costs of monolingualism cited by Snow and Hakuta (1989) are certainly also relevant to the Canadian context.

Clearly, the rationales outlined above for heritage language promotion all relate in some way to "multicultural education." In the Canadian context, however, the concept of "multicultural education" remains ill-defined in theory as well as in practice (see Mallea, 1988, for an analysis of the current status of multicultural education in Canada). Thus, it is hardly surprising that the various rationales for heritage language teaching have not been integrated within a coherent framework of multicultural education. In Australia, by contrast, a coherent framework linking language promotion with the broader goals of multicultural education has begun to emerge in the context of the Australian National Policy on Languages (Lo Bianco, 1987). In the next section we outline these theoretical and policy developments which we believe have equal relevance to the Canadian debate. Then research findings relating to various aspects of the rationale for heritage language promotion are reviewed.

Heritage Languages and Multicultural Education: Theoretical and Policy Developments in Australia

In our opinion, Canadian policy-makers, educators, and ethnocultural community groups have much to learn from recent developments in heritage language teaching in the Australian context. In the first place, in most States, heritage languages or languages other than English (LOTEs) as they are known in Australia, are taught within the regular school day at both elementary and secondary levels (with funding from national and State governments). A wide variety of bilingual programs also exist intended to promote children's cognitive development in two languages (Kalantzis, Cope, & Slade, 1989; Kalantzis, Cope, Noble, & Poynting, 1989; Lo Bianco, 1989). In addition, an extremely well-balanced and coherent framework for curriculum development and instruction in LOTEs as well as in English-as-a-second-language (ESL) has been developed that, we believe, has enormous relevance for language teaching internationally (Scarino, Vale, McKay, & Clark, 1988).

Detailed examination of these developments goes beyond the scope of this book. However, the theoretical rationale underlying the Australian National Policy on Languages is worth outlining briefly because it goes some way toward resolving "dilemmas of pluralism" that are equally apparent in the Canadian context (see Mallea, 1989). Lo Bianco (1989) notes that multicultural policies have been only partially successful in exerting a major influence on mainstream curricula in the Australian context. He attributes this to three factors:

1. The utilization of inadequate notions of culture; specifically, "culture" conceived of and transmitted as a series of inert facts about particular groups rather than as a means to understanding how cultural phenomena reflect particular social structures and serve universal human needs; in other words, the cultural knowledge transmitted should be such as to generate a critical awareness of broader socio-cultural phenomena;

2. An inability to reconcile equity and culturalist orientations; in other words, should the major goal of multicultural education be to maximize educational attainment or to promote knowledge of and pride in children's cultural background?

3. The extent to which issues of culture and language maintenance are "private" concerns of ethnic groups or of broader public relevance to the entire society.

Lo Bianco (1989) suggests that a new version of multicultural education is now emerging that has the potential to overcome these three obstacles and exert a pervasive influence over mainstream curricula. This reconceptualized multiculturalism emphasizes the role of linguistic and cultural diversity as resources of direct benefit in attaining important goals set by the society. The societal goals relate to Australia's role in the world and the potential of multiculturalism to become a domestic modelling of internationalism. Lo Bianco suggests that building on a general cultural awareness and positive appreciation of diversity in Australia would represent a significant step in the broader inculcation of internationalist consciousness.

> Multicultural education that prepares the individual for Australia's world and regional participation should also involve expansion of the cultural and identity repertoire of each student. ... It will be vital to reinforce the identity of students if we are to then ask them to go beyond it. ... The purpose of such programs ought not merely to be to reinforce or bolster self-esteem for minority children, nor simply to inculcate positive attitudes in minority and majority children, but rather to also impart cultural knowledge which is analytical and critical. (1989, p.35-36)

According to Lo Bianco, this conception of multicultural education implies a non-static notion of culture in which the skills, knowledge, and awareness children bring to school become the basis for generating a deeper understanding of culture and inter-group relations. In this way, both equity and culturalist orientations are accommodated, the former because the backgrounds of minority children assume a more positively valued role and the latter because children's cultural identity is reinforced in the process of developing a critical awareness of the deeper role that culture plays in group life. The public-private division is also addressed since the goals being advocated are clearly universal and would be accommodated in the curricula of all schools. Any private efforts organized to the same end (e.g. language teaching) would simply reinforce the general activity.

In short, the cultures and languages of minority groups, if seen as resources to be conserved, valued and built on, become cognitive and attitudinal advantages directly relevant to the self-perceived needs of the nation for a culturally and linguistically more adaptable, skilled and sophisticated population. In other words, viewing linguistic and cultural diversity as societal resources overcomes, at least in principle, the "us" and "them" perspective that has been so typical of the heritage language debates in many countries including Canada and Australia.

In the next section we elaborate on this perspective of language as an individual and societal resource by reviewing the research evidence regarding the effects of heritage language development on the individual child. We then consider the benefits for particular ethnocultural communities and for Canadian society as a whole.

Research on Bilingualism and Heritage Language Promotion

Heritage Language Development in the Home

Several studies show that the use of a minority language in the home is not, in itself, a handicap to children's academic progress. For example, a study conducted in the English-Ukrainian bilingual program in Edmonton (Cummins and Mulcahy, 1978) found that students who were most fluent in Ukrainian as a result of speaking it consistently at home were better able to detect ambiguities in English sentence structure than either monolingual English students or those who came from Ukrainian ethnic backgrounds but who used English mainly in the home. In a study conducted in Montreal among Italian background children, Bhatnagar (1980) reported that students who used both Italian and an official Canadian language (i.e. English or French) in the home were performing better in English or French of both the spoken and written variety than those who used English or French all the time. He concluded that "language retention ... should lead to higher academic adjustment, better facility in the host language, and better social relations of immigrant children" (1980, p. 155).

Similar findings have emerged from the United States context. Dolson (1985), for example, investigated the academic performance of 108 Hispanic students in grades 5 and 6 in relation to the extent that Spanish had been maintained as the major home language. He reported that students who had switched to English as their main home language performed significantly more poorly on 5 measures of English academic performance in comparison to students who had maintained Spanish as their main home language.

These findings suggest that educators should be extremely cautious in advising minority parents to use English rather than their mother tongue at home. There is no evidence that use of a heritage language at home impedes English acquisition. In fact, a switch to English by minority parents may have negative consequences for their children's conceptual and academic development in that the quality (and quantity) of interaction to which children are exposed is likely to decrease if parents are not as fluent in English as in their mother tongue. A 10-year longitudinal research study carried out by Gordon Wells (1981) in Britain (with monolingual children) shows clearly that the extent to which adults interact with their children and extend and develop the topics initiated by children is a highly significant factor in children's acquisition of academic skills in school. The data on bilingualism show that it does not matter whether this interaction is in English or in the child's mother tongue since there is considerable transfer of conceptual and academic skills across languages.

The implication of these findings is that educators should strongly encourage minority parents to interact with their children through their home language and, to the extent feasible, promote an interest among their children in books and stories. Children who come to school with this type of experience have an advantage in that they have been exposed to realities that are removed from the immediate here-and-now. They have also learned to process the language that is necessary to describe and manipulate abstract ideas, a crucial aspect of success in school.

This conclusion is reinforced by the results of a recent longitudinal study that followed Portuguese-background students in Toronto from the Junior Kindergarten (JK) (age 4) through Grade 1 (age 6) levels (Cummins, Ramos, Lopes, 1989). Loss of Portuguese language skills during this three year period was surprisingly rapid. While a large majority of the 24 children in the study were considerably more fluent in Portuguese than in English at the JK level, by grade 1 almost all the children were more fluent in English despite the fact that parents and grandparents continued to use Portuguese predominantly with them in the home. The study also found that the level of English reading skills attained by the children at the end of grade 1 was just as strongly related to preschool indices of Portuguese proficiency as to indices of English proficiency. It was concluded that academic development is related to the extent to which deeper levels of language and conceptual development are stimulated by children's interaction in the home and preschool. The specific language that is used as a medium for this stimulation is less important than the quality of the stimulation itself. However, when parents are more comfortable in the heritage language than in English or French, a higher quality of interaction is likely when that language is used as the major medium of communication in the home.

In summary, rather than potentially jeopardizing minority children's academic prospects (not to mention their potential for full bilingual proficiency) by advising parents to use English in the home, educators should encourage parents to strongly promote children's conceptual development in their mother tongue by reading to them, telling stories, singing songs, and so on. Despite the endorsement of "multicultural education" in schools systems across Canada during the past 20 years, parents from ethnocultural backgrounds continue to report that educators advise them to switch to English in the home. This is perhaps an indication of how superficially "multicultural education" has been interpreted by some faculties of education and school systems.

Heritage Language Promotion in the Preschool

Considerable international attention has been paid in recent years to the potential of preschool programs to promote the acquisition and/or maintenance of heritage languages. Such programs have spread rapidly in Europe as a means of developing a foundation in the heritage language prior to the start of formal schooling. Languages such as Irish and Scots Gaelic, Welsh, Breton, Frisian, etc, have all demonstrated newfound vitality as a result of the popularity of preschool programs conducted in the language. In New Zealand more than 500 *kohanga reo* (language nests) have been started during the past decade as a means of halting the decline of the Maori language. The *kohanga reo* accept children from the first year of life with the intent of surrounding them with the Maori language. They are supported financially by the New Zealand government and are staffed by both paid and volunteer personnel. These programs have, in turn, created pressure for the implementation of bilingual programs at the elementary level.

In Canada, privately-operated French preschool programs are relatively common in most major cities but relatively few preschool programs exist in heritage languages. The rapid decline in heritage language skills that takes place between ages 4 and 6 in regular school JK and SK programs (Cummins et al, 1989) suggests that it is important to pursue heritage language preschool programs as a viable option in the struggle to promote continued development of these language skills.

We briefly noted in the previous chapter the recently initiated Gaelic playgroup in Cape Breton, but only one heritage language preschool program has been described in detail in the Canadian research literature. This was a program initiated by the Inter-Cultural Association of Greater Victoria in cooperation with the Hindu Parishad and the Sikh Temple. The program was intended for Punjabi-speaking families with preschoolers (MacNamee and White, 1985). Sessions took place Mondays and Wednesdays for two hours of the afternoon in a local church hall used as a meeting place by the Hindu Parishad. While the children attended a preschool program supervised by a preschool teacher and members of the local Punjabi-speaking community, the adults (mostly grandparents) got together for English-as-a-second-language (ESL) instruction taught by an ESL teacher.

MacNamee and White note that the initial goal of the preschool had been to help the children take first steps in using English while stimulating and reinforcing their command of their first language. However, they found that children who already had some preschool experience did not need any help with English but had to be encouraged to use Punjabi. The children's initial unwillingness to use the home language or to discuss Indian themes also extended to an attitude of rejection towards the older people when they contributed traditional songs and stories. This attitude gradually shifted as the program continued, although it did not disappear entirely:

> By the third week, we noticed that the language balance was gradually shifting with a lot more Punjabi being used by the children in the preschool space—in play interaction, in spontaneous presentation of song and rhyme, and so on. It was found important to take a direct interest in the children's linguistic accomplishment, for with a little encouragement they provided Punjabi words for a wealth of items. That the previous preschool experiences these children have had—enriching though they may undoubtedly have been in many respects—did not come across as being supportive of a bilingual/bicultural lifestyle is suggested by an exchange that occurred during play. Two children are talking in Punjabi. A third child interjects (in English): 'No Punjabi in the school!' (1985, p. 21)

At this point the preschool teacher talked with them about how not everybody can speak two languages and how lucky they are that they can. As a result of this type of encouragement the children became more eager to talk about their language and culture.

MacNamee and White go on to discuss the fact that in successful bilingual or multilingual situations languages are maintained because they have distinct contexts and ranges of functions. A preschool program focussing on heritage language development can help establish a distinct context for the heritage language by associating it with the home environment and the ethnic community where it will not be in direct competition with the much more powerful English language. Such a program

> ...can make truly bilingual/bicultural lifestyles possible for the young by demonstrating that two languages can be learned in tandem, with the development of one contributing to the development of the other. In this way, preschool education, however alien it may be to the cultural tradition of an ethnic community such as the one involved in our programme, can be a valuable supplement to the family's efforts to implant and develop language and culture in the young child. (p. 22)

The preschool program can provide a structure whereby the ethnic community can encourage parents to interact with their children in ways that are likely to promote later school success (e.g. conversation, children's books, films and educational events in the heritage language). MacNamee and White stress, however, that the ethnic community itself must be in charge of the program. They suggest that a proliferation of ethnic preschools in Canada is neither unreasonable nor unworkable and is, in fact, a rational response on the part of communities and educators to the "astounding" evidence that "children whose language and culture are only developing can, following preschool experiences in majority-culture settings, already be rejecting their own families' language and culture" (p. 23).

An additional consideration with respect to provision of preschool bilingual programs is the demonstration that children of this age can acquire reading skills in two languages (Lado, Hanson, & D'Emilio, 1980; Titone, 1988). This idea has been investigated only on a small scale in Canada (d'Onofrio, 1988) but it merits further exploration, particularly for children who are academically at-risk.

In short, heritage language preschool programs offer considerable potential for consolidating children's conceptual foundation in their heritage language. However, at the present time this potential is being only minimally realized in Canada. As daycare programs expand, ethnocultural communities would do well to explore the feasibility of reinforcing their children's language and culture by incorporating heritage language promotion into these programs. If this does not happen, daycare/preschool programs will accelerate the already rapid demise of children's mother tongues.

Heritage Language Development in School

A review of the literature on heritage language education conducted for the Ontario Ministry of Education (Cummins, 1983) revealed that very little research had been carried out on the effects of teaching heritage languages as subjects of instruction. However, a large amount of research from Canada, the United States and many other countries is available on the effects of bilingual programs for linguistic minority students. The results of these programs are consistent in showing that the use of a heritage language for all or part of the school day entails no long-term loss in the development of academic skills in the majority language (English). This is essentially the same type of finding as in the case of French immersion programs and suggests that there is considerable transfer of academic skills across languages. Expressed differently, there is interdependence of conceptual or literacy-related skills between first and second languages.

In many cases bilingual programs have resulted in improved academic performance by minority students, and parents have become more involved in their children's education. This latter finding appeared in the evaluations of several short-lived transitional bilingual programs in Ontario in the mid-seventies (see *Appendix* for a review). For example, an Italian-English transitional program that operated at the JK and SK levels of the Toronto Board in the mid-seventies (Shapson and Purbhoo, 1977) showed that students in the program participated significantly more in class discussions than equivalent students in regular English-only classrooms. Shapson and Purbhoo suggest that

> Increased participation in class discussions may be considered a signal that the child feels comfortable and important in school. It might be viewed as an indicator of self-concept. (1977, p. 490)

They also reported that parents of children in the transition classes attended more school functions and participated more in classroom events than the comparison group parents.

Official government documents in Quebec have also reviewed in detail research related to the psychological and pedagogical rationale for heritage language promotion. These documents similarly conclude that children's proficiency in their first language provides a conceptual foundation for future academic growth in the school language. The Conseil Superieur de l'Education, for example, points out that:

> Des recherches tendent à démontrer que lorsque les élèves ne maîtrisent pas suffisamment ni leur langue maternelle ni la langue de la société d'acceuil, ils accusent du retard dans leur développement, tant en ce qui concerne leurs performances linguistiques qu'en ce qui touche à l'acquisition des connaissances. (1983, p. 40)

> (Research tends to show that when students acquire insufficient mastery of both their mother tongue and the societal language, they risk a delay in both their linguistic and conceptual development.)

There is also an acknowledgement that the time allotted to the PELCO may be insufficient in view of the needs of minority students:

> Compte tenu des besoins des élèves, le temps consacré à l'étude de la langue d'origine (30 minutes/jour) n'est peut-être pas suffisant, mais il permet au moins de renforcer certains concepts acquis en langue d'acceuil. De plus, il valorise la langue et la culture d'origine dans le cadre scolaire public.
> *(Bureau des Services aux Communautés Culturelles, 1983, p. 12)*
>
> (Given the needs of students, the time devoted to study of the heritage language (30 minutes per day) is perhaps not sufficient, but it at least allows certain concepts acquired in the major school language to be reinforced. Moreover, it valorizes the heritage language and culture within the public school system.)

The lack of sufficient time for full heritage language development when it is taught for only two and one half hours per week has led some ethnocultural communities in Ontario to argue for enrichment bilingual programs similar to those that operate in the west of Canada (e.g. Wynnyckyj, 1989a, 1989b). The evaluation results from bilingual programs in the Prairie provinces clearly demonstrate that heritage language promotion will have no adverse effects on children's overall academic development and may, in fact, enhance aspects of that development. The evaluation of the Edmonton Public School Board (EPSB) English-Ukrainian program, for example, showed that by Grade 5 students in the program who had been instructed for 50% of the time through Ukrainian were performing significantly better than the control group in both English reading and mathematics. No consistent differences had been evident in previous years. Thus, considerably less time through the medium of English resulted in no reduction in English academic proficiency. This result is analogous to that found in French immersion programs; however, unlike most French immersion programs, students in the Ukrainian bilingual program are representative of the general population both in terms of socio-economic status and ability levels (Edmonton Public Schools, 1980).

One major limitation of the heritage languages program as it has been implemented in Ontario is that the program is marginalized outside the regular education system and thus "mainstream" teachers may feel little incentive or obligation to valorize and reinforce children's first language in their interactions with children and parents. This point was noted by a Study Group from Britain who visited Toronto in 1987 in order to observe initiatives in multicultural education (Fox, Coles, Haddon & Munns, 1987). They suggest that the ambivalence over heritage language teaching in Canada is symptomatic of a more general ambivalence about anti-racist education:

> On the one hand very impressive heritage language programmes, often well run and taught, disguise the fact that these languages are not actually part of mainstream provision and can serve to marginalize the importance of the first language. School principals do not control them and some feel little ownership of them. Far from encouraging a school to build upon the language and culture that the child brings from home, the programme can serve to encourage teachers to ignore it altogether as it is being dealt with by other agencies. (1987, p. 20)

We shall suggest in a later section that the potential benefits of heritage language teaching are likely to be realized much more effectively when the program is integrated within a more general approach to the study of language and the development of language awareness. This would involve heritage language, French and English teachers encouraging students to make explicit comparisons and contrasts across languages and integrating language study with other curricular areas (e.g. the study of society and cultures).

In summary, the findings of many international evaluations suggest that bilingual heritage language programs will not hinder children's acquisition of English academic skills and may, in fact, enhance overall school performance. In other words, the endorsement of bilingual and trilingual programs in the Toronto Board's Third Languages Work Group Report (1982) has considerable research support. The way in which heritage language programs have been implemented in some provinces, however, remains problematic in that children's mother tongues have been effectively "deported" from the regular school environment leaving the educational status quo unchanged. The resulting message to the child is clear.

The Effects of Bilingualism on Intellectual and Academic Development

In the past many students from minority backgrounds have experienced difficulties in school and have performed worse than monolingual children on verbal IQ tests and on measures of literacy development. These findings led researchers in the period between 1920 and 1960 to speculate that bilingualism caused language handicaps and cognitive confusion among children. Some research studies also reported that bilingual children suffered emotional conflicts more frequently than monolingual children. Thus, in the early part of this century bilingualism acquired a doubtful reputation among educators, and many schools redoubled their efforts to eradicate minority children's first language on the grounds that this language was the source of children's academic difficulties.

However, virtually all of this early research involved minority students who were in the process of replacing their first language by the majority language, usually with strong encouragement from the school. Many minority students in North America were physically punished for speaking their first language in school. Thus, these students usually failed to develop adequate literacy skills in their first language and many also experienced academic and emotional difficulty in school. This, however, was not because of bilingualism but rather because of the treatment they received in schools which essentially amounted to an assault on their personal identities.

More recent studies show that far from being a negative force in children's personal and academic development, bilingualism can positively affect both intellectual and linguistic progress. A large number of studies have reported that bilingual children exhibit a greater sensitivity to linguistic meanings and are more flexible in their thinking than are monolingual students (see Lambert 1990 for a review).

In general, it is not surprising that bilingual children should be more adept at certain aspects of linguistic processing. In gaining control over two language systems, the bilingual child has had to decipher much more language input than the monolingual child who has been exposed to only one language system. Thus, the bilingual child has had considerably more practice in analyzing meanings than the monolingual child.

A recent study carried out by Danesi, Cicogna, Menechella, and Gaspari (in press) illustrates this pattern. Drawing on the report cards of 100 randomly chosen children of Italian background who had studied Italian as a heritage language and 100 Italian-background children who had not, the groups were compared on aspects of English language skills. Significant differences were found in English spelling skills in favour of those who had studied Italian. Again, enhancement of children's awareness of language itself represents a likely explanation of this finding.

An important characteristic of bilingual children in the more recent studies (conducted since the early 1960's) is that they are in the process of developing what Lambert (1990) has termed an additive form of bilingualism; in other words, they had added a second language to their repertory of skills at no cost to the development of their first language. Consequently, they had attained a relatively high level of both fluency and literacy in their two languages. The children in these studies tended to come from majority language groups whose first language was strongly reinforced in the society (e.g. English-speakers in French immersion programs) or from minority groups whose first languages had been reinforced by bilingual programs in the school.

For minority students, attainment of a high level of bilingual proficiency appears to depend on the extent to which the first language is developed. When conceptual skills in the first language are not well developed, many children will lack the foundation upon which to build adequate second language conceptual skills. Thus, it is extremely important for parents to reinforce the first language in the home if minority children are to develop an additive form of bilingualism.

The Effects of Bilingualism on the Learning of Additional Languages

Both research findings and anecdotal evidence suggest that minority language children acquire French more easily than children from monolingual English backgrounds. For example, in 1969 the French Department of the Toronto Board of Education observed that

> ...students who are learning French as a third language perform better than children who are learning French as a second language. Somehow the learning of a third language is facilitated by the learning of a second. *(Saif and Sheldon, 1969, p. 7)*

MacNamee and White (1985) similarly argue that "the learning of two languages immeasurably facilitates the eventual learning of a third" and they suggest that "young ethnic Canadians who have acquired and maintained their ancestral language are more likely to acquire a second official language and make it part of their adult lives in the future" (p. 23).

Some of the early research on French immersion programs carried out in Ottawa suggested that these speculations had some basis in that minority students performed well in French immersion programs (for a review see Genesee, 1976). However, these studies were not intended to directly address this question and controls for socioeconomic status were lacking.

The most direct and convincing support for the positive influence of heritage language proficiency on the learning of additional languages comes from a study of more than 300 grade 8 students in the Metropolitan Separate School Board (MSSB) French-English bilingual program conducted by Swain, Lapkin, Rowen and Hart (1988). The program starts at the grade 5 level where 50% of the student's time is spent in each language. Swain et al compared four groups of students on various measures of French proficiency: those who had no knowledge of a heritage language (HL); those with some knowledge but no literacy skills in the HL; those with HL literacy skills but who mentioned no active use of HL literacy; and finally those who understand and use the HL in the written mode. The first group had parents with higher educational and occupational status than the other three groups who did not differ in this regard.

Highly significant differences in favour of those students with HL literacy skills were found on both written and oral measures of French. There was also a trend for students from Romance language backgrounds to perform better in oral aspects of French, but the differences between Romance and non-Romance language background students were not highly significant. The authors conclude that there is transfer of knowledge and learning processes across languages and development of first language literacy entails concrete benefits for students' acquisition of subsequent languages.

In short, the research data suggest that there is considerable validity to the claim that promoting heritage language proficiency will enhance the educational development of the individual child. When children develop heritage language literacy skills they are developing not only skills in that specific language; they are also deepening their knowledge of language and literacy in general and this entails concrete benefits in other areas of academic effort.

Heritage Language Promotion as a Core Component of Multiculturalism

As indicated in previous chapters, there has been considerable discussion about the extent to which a multicultural policy necessarily entails support for heritage language promotion. We agree strongly with those who argue that multiculturalism represents little more than empty rhetoric if it does not include heritage language promotion as an integral component. This issue is clearly not amenable to empirical verification through research; rather it is a matter of individual and group convictions. The case for the inseparability of multiculturalism and heritage language promotion is clearly expressed in the following quotation taken from the submission of the Ukrainian Canadian Committee School Board (Toronto Branch) to the Ontario Ministry of Education in response to its *Proposal for Action* on the heritage language program:

> By providing a rich variety of educational experiences aimed at strengthening the child's ties to his/her family roots, traditions and culture, we allow the child to develop a sense of self-worth and self-esteem. Once the child is confident in who he/she is, he/she can share his/her knowledge and experiences with children from a variety of other backgrounds that make up the framework of Canada. In order for a child to develop and maintain a concept of self-esteem and pride in the ethnocultural traditions of his/her ancestors the child's community roots need to be reinforced within the provincial educational system. The

child's roots are not 'enrichment.' On the contrary, they are a vital part of the child's being. When viewing the entire child, it is not possible to divorce the home, the cultural roots and the general society. As a result, heritage language instruction should not be a part of continuing (enrichment) education, but a comprehensive part of the child's total educational process. (1987, p. 2)

These arguments are considerably strengthened when placed in the context of the extremely rapid degeneration of children's first language and culture within the regular school system. When children receive the clear message in the preschool, elementary school, and high school that their language and culture should be left at the school gate, then the education system has abandoned its goal of educating the entire child. The importance of language development in helping children understand their cultural roots is expressed in the following quotation from an article on the Toronto heritage language battles:

Nick Manimanakis, a Greek-speaking parent agrees. 'If you don't know your roots, you are nothing,' he says. For many immigrant families there was a strong linguistic schism between children, parents and grandparents. 'My kids now feel comfortable in the house when we speak Greek,' adds Mr. Manimanakis. 'They can talk with their grandparents and write to their relatives in Greece. That kind of confidence and pride in their roots is the most important thing we can give our kids.' *(Elwood, 1989, p. 25)*

The importance of promoting multilingualism as an essential element in the preservation of a strong fabric of cultural communities woven together across Canada was well expressed by the Commissioner of Official Languages (Max Yalden) in his 1983 report under the heading "Heritage Languages: Endangered Speeches:"

Canadians can lay claim to over a hundred languages besides English and French, each one of them with unique cultural overtones. Canada has pledged its respect to this cultural heritage but its intentions toward the languages that are its principal vehicles are uncertain. One does not have to look far or very searchingly to know that minority languages that are not given a modicum of institutional support are condemned to a more-or-less inescapable demise. ... There is no doubt that some members of the official languages communities are less than warm towards institutionalizing heritage language support. They are not against the cultural traditions that are, in part, embodied in these languages. On the contrary, so long as they are predominantly the concern of the so-called ethnic communities themselves, they are seen as enhancing our common environment. But the not always unspoken question is how far the cultivation of multiple linguistic traditions can or should be allowed to go. Unfortunately, perfectly normal doubts about the risks of social fragmentation can and sometimes do become morbid hostility toward anything different. Governments have a duty to promote social cohesion, but they also have an obligation to see that prejudice is resisted so far as possible. ... It is our belief that a decent degree of institutional and community encouragement of Canadian languages other than English and French is one way out of narrowness, timidity and conformity, which tend to sap our national potential. (1983, p. 23-24)

The Benefits of Multilingualism for Canadian Society

We live in a world that is becoming increasingly interdependent culturally, economically, environmentally, and scientifically. The ease with which information can be transmitted across the globe through telecommunications, the increasing mobility of populations, and the global impact of environmental disasters point to the need to develop among our children the desire and ability to cooperate with people from diverse linguistic and cultural backgrounds in resolving problems of global concern. Maintenance and development of language skills that Canadian children have as their birthright is clearly of direct relevance to this process of global cooperation. To deny the importance of multilingual skills and cross-cultural insights to Canada's future role in the world amounts either to chauvinism or xenophobia.

As noted earlier in this chapter, the economic and diplomatic aspects of this argument have been highlighted by a number of commentators in both the United States and Canada. These commentators have argued that the multilingual abilities that children acquire in the home represent human resources that have enormous value to the nation's economic and diplomatic endeavours. While we believe that these arguments are valid, they should not be emphasized to the exclusion of other more fundamental reasons for promoting children's linguistic skills; for example, the importance for some minority children of bilingual education for ensuring educational equity, the benefits of multilingual skills for children's cognitive development, and the role of multilingual competence in facilitating international cooperation. The danger is that some "economically-significant" heritage languages (e.g. Pacific-Rim languages in British Columbia) might receive government support while "economically-insignificant" languages are neglected. This perspective represents an extremely short-sighted and narrow orientation to heritage language promotion insofar as it ignores the importance of language to children's educational development and the fact that Canada's international role extends beyond narrow economic and diplomatic endeavours. With this caveat, we briefly review the arguments that have been advanced regarding the economic implications of promoting (and not promoting) multilingual skills among Canadian school children.

In submissions to the Ontario Ministry of Education's *Proposal for Action*, proponents of heritage language teaching frequently pointed to the relevance of children's linguistic resources for Canada's economic well-being and international effectiveness. Davis (1987) summarizes these points as follows:

> It is pointed out that benefits to Canada could result if the products of its system of education were able to meet its economic—and political—competitors on an equal footing in terms of both language ability and an understanding of the 'competitor's' prevailing culture. (p. 11)

Similar sentiments were expressed by former Northern Telecom chairperson Walter F. Light in an April 1985 speech reported in the *Canadian Parents for French Newsletter* (June 1985, p. 3). Light argued that Canada "needs to dedicate itself more strenuously to becoming a nation of world traders or risk confinement in North American markets under increasing attack from offshore competition." He went on to suggest that "we are going to have to drop the ridiculous debate on whether or not we wish to be a bilingual nation and accept that in the markets of the world multilingualism separates the winner from the losers. While, indeed, English is the universal language of commerce and of science, more deals are closed in Italy in Italian, in France in French, and in Germany in German, than are closed in English."

The same point was made with reference to Japanese by Donald Coxe in the February 1985 issue of *Canadian Business*:

> It should be obvious that any attempt to understand Japanese cultural and business practices without fluency in their language is doomed to failure. Yet we regularly read analyses of Japanese business written by people who speak no Japanese. What they do is take a month long trip to the Orient where they study various works in translation, studies that are as authoritative as articles on baseball written by cricketers. ... If Canada seriously thinks the Pacific Rim is where the economic action is and where it will be, then we need to give our young people a chance to share that action by giving them the opportunity to be fluent in the region's languages. The white man's biggest burden these days is his total ignorance of ideograms. The burden may soon become intolerable. (1985, p. 194)

In March 1984, the Multiculturalism Directorate of the federal government submitted a brief to the Royal Commission on the Economic Union and Development Prospects for Canada (the MacDonald Commission) in which the economic costs of both racial discrimination and inadequate promotion of heritage languages were discussed. The brief makes the point that although the maintenance of multiculturalism and promotion of heritage languages does cost money, it is important to recognize that the costs of not maintaining our multicultural resources are much greater in the long term. They quote from William Johnson's column in the *Globe and Mail* (12 October, 1983) in which he states:

> It has long seemed to me that we waste a valuable resource when we don't capitalize on the language proficiency of children who reach the first year of school able to speak Ukrainian, Italian, Chinese or Greek. ...To duplicate that basic competence in the school system would be expensive in time and money. But, typically, we allow that valuable initial competence to wither in the school system. We say, in effect, that Italian, German, Portuguese or Japanese are of no significance in Canadian schools. *(cited in Collenette, 1984, p. 23)*

The potential cost-effectiveness of heritage language promotion was expressed in concrete terms by Professor Odysseus Katsaitis in a submission to the Ontario Legislature on behalf of the Council of Ontario Communities. Richard Johnston, the NDP education critic, speaking on June 6, 1989, in the Ontario Legislature on the government's heritage language legislation, quoted at length from this brief. He pointed out that the government of Canada estimates the cost of training a diplomat in Japanese or sending a civil servant from Ottawa to Japan for two years to be trained in Japanese is $500,000. Similarly, the Hellenic-Canadian Federation of Ontario estimated that if just 2,000 young people from Greek heritage maintained their Greek to a level that would allow them to participate at the diplomatic or commercial level internationally, it would be worth $200 million to Canada (*Hansard*, June 6, 1989, p. 982).

In summary, the point is an obvious one. Linguistic resources are economic resources just as surely as Canada's oil or forests are. In the past ignorance and prejudice have prevented us from acknowledging this fact and even today in most provinces we promote heritage languages in much less imaginative and effective ways than we might as a result of the vested interests and political influence of some sectors of the community. In particular, the lack of valorization within the regular school classroom for linguistic and cultural diversity costs the Canadian taxpayer an enormous amount of money in squandered linguistic resources.

Summary and Conclusion

The rationale for promoting heritage languages within the public school system rests on the potential impact of such teaching on the individual child, the ethnocultural community, and Canadian society as a whole. With respect to the positive impact on the child, the research findings point to the beneficial effects of bilingualism and trilingualism for the overall educational development of the child. The personal and conceptual foundation that the child develops in her culture and language increases her sense of confidence and enhances cognitive growth and success in acquiring additional languages.

There are also strong arguments relating to the importance

of rooting children's development in a knowledge and appreciation of the culture and traditions of their ethnocultural community. Survival of the community depends on the next generation continuing to identify with it, at least in part. For children, knowledge of their heritage language unlocks not only personal contact with grandparents and, in some cases, parents, but also the collective history of the group, to which the child's own history will contribute.

These two sets of arguments clearly entail benefits for the society as a whole. Canadian society is stronger as a result of individuals who have developed rather than squandered their linguistic talents and who have a strong sense of belonging to their ethnocultural community in addition to the broader Canadian society. However, there are also tangible benefits with respect to Canada's role in an increasingly interdependent global community. Canadian society requires people who can play an active role in promoting international understanding and cooperation. This can be achieved much more effectively by individuals who speak and read several languages rather than just one. In addition, business people and diplomats with multilingual competence are increasingly in demand and development of such skills among adults can be enormously expensive. A change in attitude in our schools such that children's linguistic talents were valued and encouraged in the regular classroom together with more imaginative heritage language provision would be highly cost-effective in increasing Canada's international impact.

Clearly, social, political, administrative, and financial questions are inextricably intertwined with the issue of the educational merits of heritage language promotion. At issue is the extent to which a societal commitment to "multiculturalism" in education extends to collaborating with communities in promoting children's linguistic talents. If it does not, then it may amount to little more than a rhetorical facade obscuring an unrepentant assimilationist policy.

In the next chapter we consider one specific linguistic minority, the Deaf community, and the role of heritage language and/or bilingual programs in reversing their educational failure. This case study illustrates the central role that societal power relations have played and continue to play in determining the educational opportunities that are made available to minority children.

FOOTNOTES

[1] Extracted from SOHL brochure entitled *Heritage Languages Can Bring the World to You!* (no date).

Chapter 5

Denial of Voice
The Suppression of Deaf Children's Language in Canadian Schools[1]

In recent years, the Deaf community[2] in Canada and the United States has demanded that American Sign Language (ASL) be recognised as a valid language of instruction within the educational system. This assertion of educational rights among the Deaf community received widespread public attention in the spring of 1988 when deaf students in Gallaudet University in Washington D.C. rejected the appointment of a hearing President and forced the Board of Trustees to appoint Gallaudet's first deaf President, Dr. I. King Jordan. The fact that the only university for deaf people in North America had to wait until 1988 for a deaf person to be appointed President reflects the paternalism that has characterized the education of deaf children and adults in most countries for generations (see Lane (1984) for an excellent history of the Deaf). This paternalism is most vividly illustrated in the exclusion of deaf people from the teaching profession and in the suppression of ASL in the schools.[3] The result has been that many deaf students leave school with minimal levels of literacy in English and occupy menial jobs in the wider society.

The education of deaf children received considerable attention during 1989 in Ontario. A policy review was conducted by the Ministry of Education to consider the education of deaf children in general and specifically the most effective options with regard to medium of instruction. These range from an auditory/oral position (relying on auditory training of residual hearing, speechreading and English speech production) to the inclusion of ASL as a primary medium of instruction.

Currently in Ontario, there is acceptance of the principle that ASL can be taught as a heritage language outside the regular school day but considerably more resistance to the use of ASL as a medium of instruction for teaching regular school subject matter. Consideration of this debate can help to elucidate some of the issues underlying heritage language teaching in general: specifically, what are the causes of the educational difficulty experienced by some minority students and what is the role of first language promotion in reversing these difficulties? In other words, under what conditions is it appropriate and necessary to use the child's primary or heritage language as a medium of instruction in order to reduce the risk of school failure? We shall suggest that when children from particular minority cultural groups are not at risk of school failure it is appropriate to teach heritage languages as subjects of instruction for enrichment purposes. However, when minority group children are at risk of school failure (as is the case with Deaf, Native Canadian, and minority francophone students), then bilingual programs that employ the heritage language as a medium of instruction are indicated by the research literature. The major goal of such programs is to empower students: to restore pride in their language and cultural identity, develop confidence in their ability to succeed at school and promote the critical awareness necessary for them to take control over and transform their personal and social realities.

We will first consider the instructional options with respect to medium of instruction for deaf students. Then socio-historical aspects of the the power relations that have existed between deaf and hearing people will be considered. Finally, a framework will be presented within which educational options for deaf and other "at risk" minority children can be analyzed.

Instructional Options for Deaf Students

The auditory/oral approach emphasizes development of any residual hearing with the assistance of hearing aids and the development of speechreading skills and speech production. From the latter part of the last century until the 1970s auditory/oral approaches were used almost exclusively in the education of the deaf in North America and Europe (Lane, 1984). A major part of the rationale for these approaches was that children will use the "crutch" of sign language unless they receive intensive exposure to oral language in school.

During the past 20 years, an increasing number of programs for deaf students have come to be based on the philosophy of total communication which encourages the development of all communication modes as appropriate for the degree of hearing loss particular children experience. Total communication programs use simultaneous communication as a method. Simultaneous communication retains the auditory input and adds visual information through the use of sign English. Sign English is being used as a generic term to refer to the variety of invented systems for representing English through signs (Israelite, Ewoldt, Hoffmeister et al., 1989).

The third major option is the primary use of the manual modality (i.e. signs) involving a language other than English, namely ASL. This would involve a bilingual-bicultural education in which the culture and language of the Deaf community are recognized and validated. English would be introduced as a second language making use of the conceptual foundation built up through communication in ASL. This bilingual/bicultural approach is strongly favoured by the Deaf community in both the United States and Canada but, with some exceptions, rejected by the educational power structure, which is largely controlled by hearing professionals.

The gradual movement away from exclusively oral approaches has coincided with linguistic research that has demonstrated clearly that ASL is just as rule-governed and logical as oral English. Furthermore, it has been shown that sign language acquisition in deaf homes follows the same developmental steps as does speech and language acquisition among hearing children (see e.g. Baker & Battison, 1980).

We believe that there are compelling reasons for exploring the use of ASL as a major medium of instruction for deaf children. These include:

◆ The central role that linguistic interaction plays in developing in children a conceptual foundation for future academic growth. For profoundly deaf children who are not given the opportunity to acquire ASL in their early years, cognitive development is frequently inhibited as a result of the conceptually-limited interaction to which they are exposed. Children who do have a conceptual foundation have considerably more cognitive power to bring to the task of acquiring written and oral English than those who lack such a foundation. If much of children's mental energy in the regular classroom is taken up with the laborious task of acquiring oral English, then there is little time or mental energy left over for using language as a tool for learning and intellectual exploration. As a result of its artificial character, sign English does not exploit the possibilities of the visual medium to the same degree as ASL and thus does not constitute as adequate an instructional medium;

◆ The importance of reinforcing children's sense of pride in their cultural identity as a prerequisite for confident engagement with academic tasks; when the culture and language of the Deaf community are not validated in the classroom, students will tend to internalize these negative attributions and mentally withdraw from academic effort;

◆ The equalization of power relations between Deaf and Hearing communities that would result from using ASL as a medium of instruction and requiring that professionals involved in teaching or testing deaf students be fluent in ASL.

Permitting ASL to be taught as a heritage language for two-and-one-half hours per week outside the regular school day, while effectively excluding its use within the regular classroom, does little to address these considerations. In the first place, such a heritage language program is totally inadequate to develop a conceptual foundation that can support academic growth among deaf students; secondly, it is insufficient to promote pride in deaf language and culture given the absence of deaf role models and manifestations of deaf culture and language in the regular school program; and finally, it reinforces the power structure in the society in which the culture and language of the Deaf community continue to be subordinated.

A heritage language program to teach ASL does, however, have a potential role for hearing children who wish to acquire ASL. For example, siblings or friends of deaf children may welcome the opportunity to acquire some proficiency in the language of the Deaf community. It is also appropriate for children with some residual hearing who may be learning effectively through an auditory/oral approach.

The Deaf as a Linguistic Minority

There are strong similarities between the history and experiences of the deaf community and those of other oppressed and/or colonized minorities. Grosjean (1982), for example, notes that:

> Deaf Americans share many characteristics of other linguistic minorities in the United States: they have a language and a culture of their own; they have suffered much discrimination and prejudice in such domains as education and employment; they have adopted many of the majority's negative attitudes toward their language and culture; and many of them are—to some extent at least—bilingual. (p. 88)

However, as Grosjean points out, a major difference between deaf children and those of other linguistic minorities is that enculturation into the community and acquisition of the minority language does not take place in the home because less than ten percent of deaf children have deaf parents, and thus very few are native users of ASL. ASL is usually learned at school where peers and a few deaf adults serve as models. The resulting bilingualism among deaf students can take several forms depending on the competence developed by the student in ASL, sign English, written English, and oral English. In the past, ASL was frequently ridiculed and prohibited even outside class with the result that many deaf individuals were embarrassed to use their language in public.

Harlan Lane (1988) has pointed to the similarities between the characteristics ascribed to deaf people and those attributed to colonized populations by the colonizers:

> The list of traits attributed to deaf people is inconsistent: they are both 'aggressive' and 'submissive'; they are naive/shrewd, detached/passionate, explosive/shy, stubborn/submissive, and suspicious/trusting. The list is, however, consistently negative (p. 8).

Lane argues that these traits reflect the paternalistic posture of the hearing experts making these attributions rather than any valid characteristics of deaf people. He suggests that the perceived incompetence of deaf people is a function of a hegemonic process similar to that operating in colonial racism, as described by Memmi (1966):

a. Discover differences;

b. Valorize them to the advantage of the colonizer and the disadvantage of the colonized; and

c. Absolutize them, affirming that they are definitive and act to make them so.

A similar process has operated (and in many respects still does) in most western countries with respect to minority students that tend to experience academic failure (e.g. Black, Hispanic, and Native students in the United States; Black and Native students in Canada).

In short, there are striking sociological, linguistic and educational similarities between the situation of deaf children and that of many other groups of minority children. From a sociological perspective the deaf manifest many of the characteristics of "castelike" minorities, in Ogbu's (1978) terms, in that they have been regarded as inherently inferior by the majority society and many have internalized this sense of inferiority. Their language and culture have been devalued and suppressed at school and their school failure blamed on linguistic and intellectual deficits. As in the case of other minority groups, this educational orientation has served to screen the instruction offered to deaf students from critical examination.

Strategies for reversing the educational failure of deaf children can be considered within the context of the framework outlined in Figure 5-1.

Figure 5-1

Empowerment of Minority Students: A Framework for Intervention

SOCIETAL CONTEXT

MAJORITY GROUP	⟵————⟶	**SUBORDINATED GROUP**
	↓	
	ambivalent insecure minority group identity	

EDUCATIONAL CONTEXT

Educator Role Definitions

	INTER-CULTURAL ORIENTATION	ANGLO-CONFORMITY ORIENTATION
Cultural–Linguistic Incorporation	**Additive**	**Subtractive**
Community Participation	**Collaborative**	**Exclusionary**
Pedagogy	**Interactive–Experiential–Critical**	**Transmission**
Assessment	**Advocacy–Oriented**	**Legitimacy–Oriented**
	⟶ **EMPOWERED STUDENTS**	⟶ **DISABLED STUDENTS**

Reversing School Failure Among Deaf Children

The framework outlined in Figure 5-1 was developed to account for the educational failure of minority students and to propose an intervention model for reversing this pattern of failure. We believe that it is also largely applicable to the historical and current educational situation of deaf children.[4] The framework proposes that minority students become empowered or disabled as an immediate result of their interactions with educators in the school context. These interactions are mediated by the implicit (or explicit) role definitions that educators assume in relation to four institutional characteristics of schools. These characteristics reflect: (a) The extent to which minority students' language and culture are incorporated within the school program; (b) The extent to which minority community participation is encouraged as an integral component of children's education; (c) The extent to which the pedagogy promotes intrinsic motivation on the part of students to use language actively in order to generate their own knowledge; and finally, (d) The extent to which professionals involved in assessment become advocates for minority students as opposed to legitimizing the location of the "problem" within the student.

These patterns of interaction in schools reflect dominant-subordinated group patterns within the society at large. A central proposition of the framework is that minority students are disabled or disempowered in schools in very much the same way that their communities are disempowered in interactions with societal institutions. In each situation, the victims are made to feel that they have failed because of their own inferiority despite the best efforts of dominant group institutions and individuals to help them. Since equality of opportunity is a given, it is assumed that individuals are responsible for their own failure. This analysis implies that minority students will succeed educationally to the extent that the patterns of interaction in the school context reverse those that prevail in the society at large.

When the patterns of minority student school failure are examined within an international perspective, it becomes evident that power and status relations between minority and majority groups exert a major influence. Examples frequently given are the failure of Finnish students in Sweden (where they are a low status group) compared to their academic success in Australia where Finns are regarded as high status (see Troike 1978); similarly, Ogbu (1978) reports that low status Buraku outcasts perform poorly in Japan but as well as any other Japanese students in the United States where they are indistinguishable from other Japanese students.

In accounting for the empirical data, theorists have employed several related constructs to describe characteristics of minority groups that tend to experience school failure. Cummins (1984), for example, discusses the "bicultural ambivalence" (or lack of cultural identification) of students in relation to both the home and school cultures; similarly, Ogbu (1978) discusses the "caste" status of minorities that fail academically and attributes their failure to economic and social discrimination combined with the internalization of the inferior status attributed to them by the dominant group. Feuerstein (1979) attributes academic failure to the alienation of a group from its own culture which disrupts the process of transmission of culture from one generation to the next. In all three conceptions, minority groups tend to experience educational success when they are positively oriented towards their own and the dominant culture (Cummins), have not internalized the dominant group attribution of inferiority (Ogbu) and are not alienated from their own cultural values (Feuerstein).

Cultural/Linguistic Incorporation.

Considerable research data suggest that for minority students who are at risk of school failure, the extent to which students' language and culture is incorporated into the school program constitutes a significant predictor of academic success (for reviews see Krashen and Biber, 1988; Cummins 1983, 1989). In these situations, students' academic success appears to reflect both the more solid cognitive/academic foundation developed through intensive first language instruction and also the reinforcement of their cultural identity. The goal in educating minority students should be to add a second language and culture to their repertoire of skills rather than subtracting their first language in the process of learning their second language.

Research studies from Europe and North America have consistently shown that deaf children of deaf parents perform significantly better than deaf children of hearing parents in reading and other aspects of academic achievement (see Israelite, Ewoldt, Hoffmeister et al for a comprehensive review). However, in Sweden, Ahlgren (1982) has shown that when hearing parents of preschool deaf children learned native sign language there were no developmental differences between their children and those of deaf children born to deaf parents. In both Sweden and Denmark where bilingual education involving native sign language is established policy, deaf children commonly attain levels of academic development comparable to those of their hearing peers (Ahlgren, 1982; Hansen, 1987). Musselman, Lindsay & Wilson (1988) have also reported that parents who used a relatively complete simultaneous communication with their preschool children (Sign English and auditory/oral input) performed at a similar level to parents using ASL. The crucial point is that communication between adults and children be sufficient in both quantity and quality to stimulate language and conceptual development. Frequently, however, when parents use simultaneous communication the signed encoding of the spoken message is incomplete. For example, Swisher (1984) reported that mothers who had been using simultaneous communication for at least two years deleted an average of 40.5% of the signs from their utterances.

A similar criticism has been made of the use of simultaneous communication in the classroom. Frequently, significant portions of the signed forms necessary to match the spoken utterance are deleted and producing sign supported speech is cumbersome for both teachers and deaf children alike (see Israelite, Ewoldt, Hoffmeister et al, 1989). Total Communication programs that rely on sign English have tended to be more more successful than exclusively auditory/oral approaches (Rudser, 1988) but they have not eliminated the educational difficulties of deaf children. Lane (1988) is scathing in his assessment of sign English and its roots in ethnocentric paternalism:

> This ethnocentric misunderstanding about the nature and status of sign language leads teachers to 'fix up' the children's 'arbitrary gestures' to make them more like English. New signs are invented by hearing people for English function words and suffixes that have no place, of course, in American Sign Language, and the grammatical order of the signs is scrambled in an attempt to duplicate English word order. No deaf child has ever learned such a system as a native language and indeed could not, for it violates the principles of the manual-visual channel of communication. No deaf adult uses such ways of communicating. But the system is widely used in classrooms with the claim that it assists the deaf child in learning English. Deaf children characteristically do not succeed in learning English, however, (Allen, 1986), so that cannot be the real reason for imposing a manual form of English on them; the ethnocentrism of paternalism is a more likely explanation. (1988, p. 10)

In short, there is no educational reason not to use ASL as a medium of instruction for deaf children and many reasons supported by both research and theory, to adopt it as soon as possible. Some North American schools are beginning to incorporate ASL as a partial medium; for example, the Alberta School for the Deaf has a policy that ASL shall be utilized to enhance communication where necessary and in the interpretation of artistic, musical, dramatic, poetic and cultural expression (personal communication Joe McLaughlin). Schools for the Deaf in Indianapolis, Delaware, Vermont, and Fremont California are also moving in the direction of using ASL as a medium of classroom instruction (Valli, Thumann-Prezioso, Lucas, Liddell, & Johnson, 1989).[5]

Community Participation.

The framework proposes that students from subordinated minorities will be empowered in the school context to the extent that the communities themselves are empowered through their interactions with the school. When educators involve minority parents as partners in their children's education, parents appear to develop a sense of efficacy that communicates itself to children with positive academic consequences.

The situation is complicated in the case of deaf children in that a large majority of parents of deaf children are not themselves members of the Deaf community and do not use ASL. Many parents resist the use of ASL in the classroom because they fear "losing" their child to the Deaf community. Their goal is to have their child develop as "normally" as possible and become as competent as possible in expression and understanding of spoken English. Intensive exposure to English in school appears to be the most logical way of doing this whereas the use of ASL appears counter-productive in that it dilutes children's exposure to English. These views are frequently reinforced by educators of the deaf who are themselves hearing and not fluent in ASL.

As we have seen the empirical data do not support these views. Parents who wish their children to develop their conceptual and academic potential should attempt to acquire at least some sign language so that they can support their children's development during the crucial preschool years. Clearly, societal institutions should provide the funds and facilities to permit hearing parents who so wish to acquire ASL and/or sign English. One such program for deaf children and their parents is operated by the Deaf Children's Society of Vancouver and has been evaluated as highly successful in facilitating both parent-child communication and social competence among children and in reducing maternal stress (Greenberg and Calderon, 1984).

A further complication in the case of deaf children is that in major North American cities, an increasing proportion of parents speak a language other than English at home. For example, in the United States between 1973/74 and 1981/82, the proportion of Hispanic students in residential schools for the hearing-impaired increased from 6.8% to 9.5%, an increase of 40% (Delgado, 1984). These students appear to experience greater academic difficulties than hearing-impaired children from English-backgrounds. Delgado (1984), for example, reported that a much higher proportion of hearing-impaired students from non-English-background homes were reported to have additional handicapping conditions. In a survey conducted in New York City, Lerman (1976) found that a disproportionate number of Hispanic students were placed in the low achieving or learning disabled groups in programs for the hearing-impaired. The picture that emerges from these surveys is one of double disadvantage for hearing-impaired children from minority groups.

An instructional approach based on sign English or oral English may create confusion for deaf students from non-English language backgrounds since parents may use a different language at home. Thus, students may be attempting to apply English speechreading strategies when Spanish or some other language is actually being used. A number of programs in the United States attempt to respond to aspects of community linguistic diversity by offering bilingual/bicultural approaches that involve languages other than English as well as ASL (e.g. the Pennsylvania School for the Deaf).

In short, because interaction in the preschool years is so crucial for children's later conceptual and personal development, parents should be encouraged and supported in acquiring proficiency in some form of signed communication, preferably ASL. Involvement of members of the Deaf community in promoting more effective communication between parents and children is clearly necessary and important in this process. Policy-makers and professional educators of the deaf should play a major role in establishing this collaboration between parents of deaf children and the Deaf community. In other words, structures should be created to facilitate both parental and Deaf community involvement in the education of deaf children. The major structural change required entails appointing more deaf individuals to positions of power in relation to the education of deaf children (e.g. as teachers, administrators and policy-makers). For parents to want to learn ASL, and to want their children to learn ASL, the status of the Deaf community must be elevated from its previously subordinated position. Fruitful collaboration between educators, parents and the Deaf community is unlikely to take place as long as deaf individuals are regarded as "deficient" by members of the dominant group, whether they be parents of deaf children or professional educators.

Pedagogy.

In the past, traditional approaches to curriculum and instruction emphasized the transmission of skills and knowledge to students whose role was to internalize this input without questioning its relevance to their lives. While Canadian school board policies have shifted significantly towards "whole language" or "interactive/experiential" approaches to curriculum and instruction in recent years, classroom practice in many contexts remains transmission-oriented. This is hardly surprising in view of the fact that transmission approaches still tend to predominate in the education of teachers in Faculties of Education.

The problem with transmission approaches for subordinated minority students is that the curriculum tends to reflect the priorities and values of the dominant group and no opportunity is given for students to use written and oral language actively to express their unique experiences. Thus, the students' language, culture and experience are seldom validated in the classroom.

The education of deaf students appears to have been so focused on transmitting oral and sign English that, in many cases, the purpose of developing students' language as a tool for communication, critical thinking and intellectual exploration has been forgotten. As Ada (1988), Giroux (1988) and other theorists of critical pedagogy point out, students can become empowered educationally only when they are encouraged to express their reality actively in the classroom; in other words, to use language to interact with others, to share their experiences, to reflect critically on these experiences and on issues in their expanding worlds, and to act creatively to exert a positive impact on their worlds. It is only through this exercise of "voice" that students can develop a sense of personal efficacy and academic confidence.

Assessment.

As outlined in Chapter 2, the indiscriminate use of biased ability and achievement tests contributed substantially to blaming the victim in the education of minority students (Ryan, 1976). Minority students' educational difficulties were attributed at various times to intrinsic characteristics of the students' themselves or their communities such as "bilingualism", "cultural deprivation," "linguistic deficits" and "genetic inferiority". These attributions operated to focus critical scrutiny away from the ways in which the interactions between minority students and educators in schools were contributing to school failure.

Lane (1988) points to serious flaws in research studies purporting to show deaf individuals to be inferior on a variety of cognitive and personality measures:

> Because the literature on the 'psychology of the deaf' is so gravely flawed by weaknesses in test administration, language, scoring, content, norms, and subject groups, many in the professions serving deaf people have sounded the alarm that the field is improperly lending the weight of science to common stereotypes. (1988, p. 16)

Other researchers have similarly noted problems in achievement tests administered to deaf students (e.g. Ewoldt, 1987). Valid assessment procedures for deaf and other minority students must move from legitimating the location of "the problem" within the student to an "advocacy" orientation that scrutinizes critically the social and educational context within which the student has developed. In other words, a primary focus of the assessment process should be on remediating the educational interactions that minority students experience.

Conclusion

The research showing that ASL is as valid a language as any other and that deaf students' first language conceptual proficiency can provide a strong foundation for the acquisition of English academic skills strongly supports the use of ASL as a medium of instruction, for reasons similar to those discussed with reference to other minority groups. However, even more fundamental than the academic reasons for bilingual instruction involving ASL, are reasons related to deaf students' cultural identity. For educators to deny deaf students the opportunity to maintain or acquire ASL essentially represents an attempt at cultural genocide, since the only identity option offered to students is to become a stigmatized member of the majority society. It is highly unfortunate that even today many schools for the deaf do not attempt to strengthen the transmission of culture by promoting ASL and helping students to integrate into the Deaf community and participate as equals within the wider hearing society. Confidence in the validity and strength of one's own culture is a necessary condition for deaf and other minority groups to fully participate in the mainstream society and demand rights of access and educational equity long denied by the dominant group.[6]

FOOTNOTES

[1] Discussions with Hartley Bressler, Carolyn Ewoldt, Neita Israelite, Gary Malkowski, Connie Meyer, Patricia Shores-Herman and Norma Jean Taylor contributed substantially to this chapter. We would also like to thank J. Boshes, Dave Mason and Joe McLaughlin for written comments on earlier drafts of this chapter. We are extremely grateful to them for their comments and criticism but we remain responsible for any errors of fact or interpretation that may remain.

The inclusion of this chapter in a book on heritage languages was motivated by the discussion in Ontario during 1989 as to whether American Sign Language (ASL) should be taught as a heritage language outside the regular school day or used as a fully legitimate medium of instruction. It seemed to us that many of the sociological and psychological issues regarding the education of minority students that we wanted to highlight were very clearly illustrated in both the history and current debates about deaf education. Neither of us, however, make any claim to being "experts" in either ASL or deaf education. We base our brief review on the existing research literature, especially the excellent survey carried out by Israelite, Ewoldt, Hoffmeister et al (1989), and try to highlight the paternalistic way in which decision-makers from the dominant group believe that they know best what is good for minority groups (in this case the Deaf) regardless of what the research evidence indicates.

2 Throughout this chapter the term "Deaf" is capitalized when it refers to the Deaf community while "deaf" is used for individuals who have a hearing loss.

3 In Canada, only 6.4% of teachers of the Deaf are themselves deaf (Israelite, Ewoldt, Hoffmeister et al, 1989).

4 Clearly, caution must be exercised in generalizing frameworks developed to account for data from one group (e.g. hearing minority students) to the situation of other groups (e.g. deaf minority students). We are suggesting that despite the obvious differences between deaf education and that of hearing minorities, there are also striking similarities in the patterns of language suppression and rationalization of students' school failure that merit exploration. While the framework does not specify the exact types of intervention that might be appropriate, it does identify general principles of intervention that we believe are applicable to the education of deaf as well as hearing children.

5 One indication of the political pressure building up within the Deaf community for a switch to ASL is the open letter to the Gallaudet Campus community written by Valli et al (1989) that calls for the full-scale adoption of ASL as the medium of instruction in Gallaudet rather than Sign Supported Speech. The authors of this letter acknowledge that although Total Communication represented a very real victory over oralism, it has not resulted in major achievement gains among deaf students due to the fact that for deaf people it is a cumbersome means of communication in which a considerable amount of information is frequently lost. [We are grateful to Hartley Bressler for sharing this letter with us.]

6 In late December 1989, the Ontario Minister of Education, Mr. Sean Conway, released the findings of the *Review of Ontario Education Programs for Deaf and Hard-of-Hearing Students*. This report endorsed the implementation of bilingual programs involving ASL. An affirmative action program to increase the number of deaf and hard-of-hearing teachers in Ontario schools was also recommended. The Deaf community in Ontario, however, was unhappy with what they perceived as delaying tactics on the part of the Ministry with respect to implementing the recommendations of the reports.

As reported by French (1989) in the *Globe and Mail*:

> Deaf activists were happy with the external review report because it supported most of the recommendations made by their own advisory committee last May. But they were not pleased with Mr. Conway's timetable for implementation, which promised further study and suggests further delay. (1989, A16)

Gary Malkowski, head of the task force on education for the Ontario Association of the Deaf, expressed his frustration with the proposed implementation delays by asking "What more can he [Conway] possibly want? Maybe he wants to see deaf children continue to suffer" (cited in French, 1989).

Chapter 6

Multiculturalism and Multilingualism in the 21st Century
Trail-Blazing or Star-Gazing?

Global migration trends, the rapid expansion of international trade and the continuing impact of high-technology communications suggest that, sooner or later, most countries around the world will have to learn how to become comfortable with diversity inside their borders. Canada, having been a multicultural society since its earliest days, has the advantage of long experience in what seems bound to become a mandatory 21st century skill: constructive co-existence among culturally and racially diverse communities. Indeed, the term 'multiculturalism' is a Canadian creation. Canadians are to enter the 21st century as the world's best prepared country, enjoying an important advantage over her friends and competitors. This is the Ottawa Government's rationale for introducing the Canadian Multiculturalism Act. ... The Canadian Government believes that, in the next century and beyond it, multiculturalism will also become a successful Canadian export as other nations adopt Canadian-style policies to achieve social harmony within their own borders. (*VOX*, 1988, no. 1, p. 20)

This expression of the refurbished official rhetoric on Canadian multiculturalism appeared in an article entitled "Canada: Trail Blazing Again?" written for the first issue of *VOX*, the journal of the Australian Advisory Council on

Languages and Multicultural Education (AACLAME). The short article was submitted originally without the question mark, suggesting that Canada's "trail blazing" initiatives in the area of multiculturalism should be accepted as a matter of fact. However, the question mark appended to the title when it appeared in print suggested that the journal editors considered this claim to be at least subject to discussion.

Certainly, as far as rhetoric is concerned, Canada can legitimately claim to be on the leading edge with respect to multiculturalism. As we have seen, however, the reality is more complex. While there are many very worthwhile initiatives at federal, provincial and local policy levels, there are also areas where Canadian policies have been characterized by a lack of vision and imagination. For example, there has been minimal exploration of bilingual education programs designed to improve the academic achievement of minority group students who tend to experience school failure (e.g. Native students). This contrasts with the widespread (but controversial) implementation of such programs in the United States and Sweden. Similarly, enrichment bilingual and trilingual programs involving heritage languages have been implemented only in private schools (e.g. Hebrew, Greek and Armenian schools in Quebec) and in the public schools of the prairie provinces; however, many examples of successful trilingual education exist in Europe and elsewhere (see below) that illustrate the feasibility of instituting alternative schools within the public system designed to provide an enriched language learning experience for students. There has not been a will in English Canada to advance beyond French immersion and further expand children's language repertoires. Finally, Canadian policy-makers have shut their eyes to the daily reality of discriminatory psychological testing of minority children. Despite the fact that litigation and legislation in the United States have repeatedly addressed problems of discriminatory testing during the past 20 years, only lip-service has been paid to the issue in Canadian educational policies.

The reason why these (and other) issues have not been addressed is that there has been relatively little political pressure to do so. Ethnocultural groups have generally been content with provision as it exists and only a small minority of communities outside the prairie provinces have pressured for full bilingual or trilingual programs involving heritage languages or shown concern about biased testing of minority students. It is probably unfair to expect most politicians to have any educational vision that goes beyond politics, still less to show leadership in attempting to implement visionary programs; however, in the absence of this vision and leadership, political expediency will continue to determine the kinds of programs that get implemented and the educational outcomes of these programs will seldom be commensurate with the enormous dedication and effort expended by teachers and communities.

In all of this, Canada's failures are no worse than those of most other countries. In fact, on the whole, many Canadian policies and programs in relation to cultural and linguistic diversity compare well with those of other OECD countries. For example, in Britain, there is minimal government support (either philosophical or financial) for heritage language teaching, and British educators and community groups frequently express admiration for Canadian initiatives in this regard.

Our major criticism of Canadian heritage language (and more broadly multicultural) provision is that (a) it is much less imaginative and effective than it might easily be, and (b) there is a smugness about Canadian "enlightenment" in all things multicultural that prevents us from exploring alternative forms of provision, and learning from the experience of other countries.

This smugness is most easily seen in the hypocritical way we brush off both our racist history and the continuation of institutionalized discrimination in Canadian society. For example, the passage quoted above implies that Canada has always been a "trail blazer" with respect to multiculturalism despite the reality of historical oppression against many ethnic groups and the continued racial discrimination against Black and Native communities. These uncomfortable facts are seldom allowed to intrude into the official rhetoric which claims that Canada has been "a multicultural society since its earliest days" and has "long experience in constructive co-existence among culturally and racially diverse communities."

The rapid global changes alluded to in the opening quotation certainly represent a national and international context that adds urgency to the multicultural endeavour. However, up to this point, Canadian schools have succeeded much better in encouraging students to relinquish rather than maintain their culture and language. The continued opposition by many professional educators to the "mainstreaming" of heritage language provision suggests that this assimilationist orientation remains dominant in many Canadian schools.

In the next section we briefly sketch the rapidly changing context of education in the 21st century and then consider the educational changes we believe are important to explore if Canada is serious about going beyond a mere flirtation with multiculturalism and global education. We argue that the multiple challenges of the 21st century can be met only if students learn to cooperate across cultural and linguistic boundaries in exploring issues and problems that are of mutual concern. In other words, we need global education programs that will prepare students to function in multilingual/multicultural contexts both nationally and internationally. This requires that all educators search for creative ways to deepen students' understanding of culture and extend their knowledge of languages. Language and culture must become mainstream; they can no longer be deported "outside the regular five-hour school day." In other words, we will attempt to specify the type of school program that responds at more than a rhetorical level to the cultural, economic, scientific and environmental realities of the 21st century.

The Rapidly Changing Context of Education

With respect to cultural realities of the 21st century, we are faced with much greater inter-cultural contact and increasing linguistic diversity within Canada as a result of the need to significantly increase immigration to avert a decline in the Canadian population. Statistics Canada estimates that immigration would need to rise to 250,000 annually just to keep the Canadian population from declining. In order to increase the population by 1% per year, considered desirable in view of our aging population, Canada would need to increase annual immigration to 650,000, almost four times our current level of 160,000. This domestic increase in cultural and linguistic diversity suggests that multilingual skills will become highly important in a variety of social service areas (e.g. hospitals) that attempt to meet the needs of a diverse population. Internationally, population mobility and much greater global interdependence, both economically and politically, have also highlighted the need to develop more effective directions for promoting cross-cultural cooperation and understanding.

Within this context, heritage language provision cannot be viewed as peripheral to mainstream schooling. The learning of languages, deepening of cultural understanding, and development of language awareness are central to the overall goals of education for the 21st century.

With respect to economic realities, the technological revolution that is currently underway has transformed the nature of the workplace. A far higher level of literacy and technical skills will be required of employees in the economy of the 1990's than was the case in the 1970's. The concern with "functional illiteracy," which is estimated to cost the Canadian economy $10 billion annually, is the result of these changing economic and employment realities rather than any real decline in literacy. Nevertheless, the implication of these changes is that any school that aims to prepare students to function within the economy of the 21st century must actively engage students in projects that develop literacy skills in the context of changing technological realities. In this context, the consistent relationship that many research studies have demonstrated between minority students' literacy development in their first language and success in acquiring literacy in the major school language (Cummins, 1984) suggests that effective forms of heritage language teaching can contribute to students' general cognitive and academic success.

In addition, the economies of the world are becoming increasingly interdependent (for better or worse) with the result that there is greater cross-national contact in the workplace. Again, at both managerial and shop floor level, the ability to work cooperatively across linguistic, cultural and racial boundaries is becoming more relevant.

With respect to scientific realities, schooling for the 21st century should seriously address the implications of the current knowledge explosion. For example, Patricia Cross (*Phi Delta Kappan*, 1984, p. 172) has pointed out that

> Between 6,000 and 7,000 scientific articles are written each day, and information doubles every five and a half years. By the time the average physician completes his or her training, half of all the information acquired in medical school is obsolete.

This changing scientific reality implies that schools should focus not on the internalization of socially-neutralized and soon-to-be-obsolete facts but on developing in students skills of accessing, critically interpreting and creatively applying information that is required for completion of particular projects or activities. Although English is currently the major international language of science and technology, knowledge of additional languages is clearly an asset both in accessing information and engaging in cooperative projects that apply this information.

With respect to environmental realities, a perusal of virtually any newspaper anywhere in the world will quickly show the extent of environmental deterioration and the enormity of the global problems that our generation has created for our children's generation to resolve. Yet, in the majority of schools across the continent, the curriculum has been sanitized such that students rarely have the opportunity to discuss critically, write about or act upon issues that directly affect the society they will form. Still less do they have the opportunity to cooperate with students from different cultural and/or linguistic groups in Canada or other parts of the world in exploring resolutions to these issues.

In summary, in order to respond to a global reality that is becoming much more interdependent culturally, economically, scientifically, and environmentally, schools should focus on developing in students abilities to access and critically evaluate information that can be applied to the resolution of problems in cooperation with students from very different cultural and linguistic backgrounds.

One significant initiative that incorporates all of these dimensions is computer networking where students from very different parts of the world (e.g. Spanish-speaking students in Toronto and Argentina) use telecommunications to cooperatively research particular phenomena (e.g. exploring Spanish proverbs used in different Spanish-speaking communities or investigating the water quality in different communities [see Cummins & Sayers, in press]). Modern technological advances open up enormous possibilities for student international cooperative projects that would simultaneously stimulate critical thinking, second language abilities and cross-cultural sensitivity. The payoff from such projects is likely to be much greater for both students and teachers when the communication is not limited to only one language.

The Role of Heritage Language Promotion in Global Education

In the sections below we briefly sketch directions for change that go beyond the rhetoric of "multiculturalism" and respond to the changing social and educational realities of the next century. First we discuss structural changes at preschool, elementary and secondary levels aimed at developing trilingual abilities and an understanding of language and cultural diversity. Then changes required to promote an intercultural/anti-racist mindset within the "regular" classroom and in the assessment process will be outlined.

Structural Changes Required for Promotion of Trilingualism

The Preschool Level.

If Canadian educators, policy-makers, and ethnocultural communities are serious about heritage language development, then provision must start at the preschool level. The extremely rapid decline in first language competence during the early school years (JK—grade 1) was demonstrated among Portuguese students in the Toronto area (Cummins, Ramos, & Lopes, 1989) and the experience of many parents and heritage language teachers also shows just how fragile children's first language abilities are. For a large majority of children born in Canada or who arrive prior to school, acquisition of fluency in English is not problematic; however, maintenance of the first language is extremely problematic. As daycare programs (conducted in English or French) expand across the country, they will be yet another force contributing to the destruction of the first language.

Canadian early childhood educators and ethnocultural communities have much to learn from the experience in Europe and New Zealand with heritage language preschool programs (termed *kohanga reo* or "language nests" in New Zealand). These programs have proved highly effective in developing heritage language abilities regardless of whether the heritage language is spoken in the home (see also Arnberg, 1987; de Jong, 1986; Sarkar, 1988; and Saunders, 1982). As we have outlined in previous chapters, a handful of heritage language preschool programs have been implemented and documented in Canada, but this type of provision does not appear to be a strong priority among ethnocultural communities or early childhood educators.

A first step in changing this situation is for ethnocultural communities and heritage language associations to discuss the feasibility of such preschool programs in particular areas and then to explore the possibilities of financial support from provincial and/or federal sources.

Elementary Level.

The bilingual programs in the prairie provinces have operated successfully for more than 15 years and demonstrate the educational feasibility of such programs both for heritage language maintenance and acquisition. Similarly, the trilingual Hebrew, French and English programs in Quebec have been evaluated as highly effective in developing trilingualism (e.g. Genesee, Tucker, & Lambert, 1978a, 1978b). The resistance to such programs in other parts of Canada, particularly Ontario, is often rationalized on the grounds that bilingual and trilingual programs are not feasible in situations where there are a large number of languages (see Hansard, 6 June 1989, p. 975).

This objection ignores the fact that most ethnocultural groups have not demanded bilingual programs and probably only a small minority would pursue this option, were it available (Davis, 1987). Even in the prairie provinces, some of the bilingual programs have had difficulty maintaining enrolments at a viable level. In Ontario, this relative lack of demand is sometimes cited as a reason for not changing the legislation to permit trilingual programs to operate. In other words, policy-makers wish to have it both ways: they refuse to allow trilingual programs both because the demand from up to 76 different language groups would be too great and also because there is insufficient demand for such programs.

The reality is that students are being denied access to the only program option that has any consistent research backing in developing heritage language literacy and fluency. We see no valid educational or political reason why school boards should not be allowed to offer alternative bilingual and/or trilingual programs to address both the aspirations of their client groups and the realities of our societal needs in the 21st century. Our estimation is that in a city like Metropolitan Toronto relatively few ethnocultural groups would avail of such options. This is precisely the nature of all alternative programs (e.g. French immersion programs). Those groups that might enrol their children in such programs would probably include Ukrainian, Armenian, Jewish, Greek, Chinese and Italian communities. Within most other communities the present heritage language provision is viewed as being reasonably appropriate.

One example of both the feasibility and success of multilingual programs is the European Schools model (Baetens Beardsmore & Kohls, 1988; Baetens Beardsmore & Lebrun, in press; Baetens Beardsmore & Swain, 1985). The European Schools system is designed to support the development of the child's mother tongue and develop proficiency in up to three additional languages. They were originally designed to meet the needs of employees of the European Economic Community who were working in countries other than their home country but are also open to non-civil servant children; several of the schools have substantial numbers of children of immigrant workers. The schools are government funded and have operated since 1958, servicing more than 12,000 students in five countries.

The schools consist of a five year primary section and a seven year secondary section, the whole forming an integrated mixed-ability (non-streamed) school. The larger schools can contain up to nine linguistic sub-sections representing the nine official languages of the European Community member states. Most of the instruction takes place in the child's first or dominant language with native speaker teachers. Right from the beginning of the program students are required to take instruction in a vehicular language which is selected from English, French or German and is different from the major instructional language. From the third year onwards, the program contains European Hours which are conducted in one of the vehicular languages which may or may not be the second (vehicular) language selected by the student. The primary goal of these European Hours is to bring together children from different sub-sections in groups of about 20 so as to integrate the population and gradually build up a European awareness and identity. The amount of instruction provided in a language other than the student's first language rises to about 25% of the total instructional time during the last three years of primary school. In the secondary program the amount of instruction provided in languages other than the first language amounts to about 50% of the program by the third year of secondary school and a third language is also mandatory by this stage.

Models similar to the European Schools system have been proposed in Canada (for example, Blake, Brouwer, & Patrick, 1989). For example, in the mid-1980s the principal of Gateway School in the North York Board of Education (Gerry Brouwer) initiated a proposal to the Board for a trilingual program in the school that would have involved Greek-English and Cantonese-English bilingual streams as well as the regular English program. The program would have been tolerated by the Ministry of Education under the provision that a language other than English or French can be used for transitional purposes in order to help children achieve academically while they are learning English, even though the intent of the proposal was enrichment rather than transition. However, the proposal was unceremoniously shot down by the trustees who saw it as leading to ghettoization of the community.

Blake, Brouwer, & Patrick (1989) have elaborated a model based on the original Gateway proposal and the European

Schools experience that would involve several schools with adjacent attendance areas offering a variety of bilingual options. For example, each school would offer the regular English language program with core French instruction. One of the schools would also offer a French immersion option and a bilingual heritage language option (e.g. Greek-English) with core French. Other schools in the group would offer different languages as bilingual options depending on the ethnic composition of their communities and the degree of interest. Children living within the attendance areas of the four schools would have the option of attending any of the schools depending on the specific program their parents wished them to attend. Children from English-speaking backgrounds would also be encouraged to enrol in the bilingual options.

Models such as this are supported by research, feasible from both an administrative and financial point of view, and offer enrichment options for children and communities not available within the regular system. Financially, there would be start-up costs for materials and curriculum development in different languages but there would be no cost for an add-on teacher (as in the current heritage language program) since the "regular" classroom instruction is delivered through the heritage language by a trained teacher fluent in that language.

The refusal by the Ministries of Education and by various school boards to encourage this type of program reveals a very limited perspective on multiculturalism and a myopic vision of Canada's role in the global community of the 21st century.

Secondary Level.

Alternative programs are equally viable at the secondary level. Just as there are secondary schools that specialize in the arts, or in science and technology, there could be secondary schools that specialize in language enrichment. All students in these schools would be expected to take instruction in English, French and at least one additional language, several of which might be offered in any particular school. The goal would be not only to encourage students to develop skills in an additional language but also to further deepen their understanding of how language works and their love of language. These schools might be conceived as schools specializing in global education and students might use telecommunications to engage in collaborative projects with students in different parts of the world, making use of and developing their language skills in the process. Student exchanges with peers in other countries might also be built into the program.

The fact that programs such as this are virtually non-existent in the Canadian context suggests that political and administrative expediency rather than educational vision dominates much of our educational practice. As Mary Ashworth (1988) has noted:

> The benefits of bilingualism are many. What is needed now is the will to establish effective programs in bilingual education and heritage language learning. (p. 202)

Promotion of Heritage Language Skills as a Component of Anti-Racist Education

A central assumption of the "empowerment" framework presented in Chapter 5 is that implementation of anti-racist educational changes requires personal redefinitions of the way in which classroom teachers and other educators interact with children and communities they serve. Suppression of children's languages and cultures has been a major way in which institutionalized racism has manifested itself within the educational system. Thus, reversal of this pattern requires that educators seek creative ways of motivating children to maintain their first language and reinforcing children's personal confidence in their cultural identity.

When heritage language provision is rigidly separated from the "regular" classroom, then teachers often feel that children's first language is of no concern to them. This is unfortunate because it may communicate to children that their first language has no place in the school or in their education. Schools, however, can play a significant role in encouraging children to develop their first language proficiency even in situations where bilingual education or heritage language teaching is not possible. Some of the ways in which schools can create a climate that is welcoming to minority parents and, at the same time, promotes children's pride in their linguistic talents have been noted by New Zealand educators (New Zealand Department of Education, 1988):

◆ Reflect the various cultural groups in the school district by providing signs in the main office and elsewhere that welcome people in the different languages of the community;

◆ Encourage students to use their first language around the school;

◆ Provide opportunities for students from the same ethnic group to communicate with one another in their first language where possible (e.g. in cooperative learning groups on at least some occasions);

◆ Recruit people who can tutor students in their first language;

◆ Provide books written in the various languages in both classrooms and the school library;

◆ Incorporate greetings and information in the various languages in newsletters and other official school communications;

◆ Provide bilingual and/or multilingual signs;

◆ Display pictures and objects of the various cultures represented at the school;

◆ Create units of work that incorporate other languages in addition to the school language;

◆ Encourage students to write contributions in their first language for school newspapers and magazines;

◆ Provide opportunities for students to study their first language in elective subjects and/or in extracurricular clubs;

◆ Encourage parents to help in the classroom, library, playground, and in clubs;

◆ Invite second language learners to use their first language during assemblies, prizegivings, and other official functions;

◆ Invite people from ethnic minority communities to act as resource people and to speak to students in both formal and informal settings.

Some of these strategies are already operating in some Canadian schools. For example, Lord Dufferin school in the Toronto Board of Education has accumulated a significant number of books in students' first languages and students are encouraged to read these books in class and bring them home for reading with parents. The East York Board of Education is also instituting a similar program in several of its schools.

However, in most school systems across Canada there has been little concerted effort to explore strategies for valorizing minority children's first language and encouraging its development. Whereas "multiculturalism" is seen as relevant to the school, heritage language development is typically regarded as a community concern. Thus, language diversity has either been ignored in the classroom or subtly discouraged. This contrasts with Britain where several projects have focussed on developing an awareness and appreciation of language diversity among all children within the regular classroom (e.g. Raleigh, 1981). Language concerns appear to have been more successfully integrated with other curricular subjects in the British multilingual classroom than in its Canadian equivalent (Fox et al, 1987).

The exclusion of children's first language from the classroom also has unfortunate consequences for the assessment of children's progress. As noted in Chapter 2, psychological assessment of minority children's academic potential is problematic when the assessment is conducted exclusively through English (or French in Quebec). Teachers, also, may be led to inappropriate conclusions in their assessment of children's classroom progress. This is illustrated by an incident recounted by a heritage language teacher who taught in an integrated Chinese program in the City of Toronto. Because a recently arrived grade 1 Chinese-background student was experiencing difficulty grasping certain concepts in math, the regular program teacher felt that he should spend time working on math rather than attend the Heritage Language class on that particular day. This upset the child considerably, and after the intervention of the heritage language teacher, the regular program teacher agreed to permit the child to attend the heritage language class. The heritage language teacher volunteered to spend some time working with the child on math during the class. It took only a few minutes to explain the math concepts to the child in Chinese after which the child understood them. The difficulty was with the language rather than with the concepts themselves (personal communication, Dorothy Chin).

This anecdote illustrates the desirability of closer cooperation between regular program and heritage language teachers in both the instructional and assessment process. At a more formal level, heritage language teachers might contribute to the assessment of children's potential by observing the child's academic and language development in the heritage language either in the context of the heritage language class or through interview techniques and discussions with parents.

The general point is that speakers of the minority child's first language are potentially valuable resource people whose linguistic and cultural experience and insights have not been effectively utilized to this point in the psychological and educational assessment process. Clearly, adequate training of such resource people should be a prerequisite to any involvement in student assessment. The fact that only a handful of school systems across Canada (e.g. The North York Board of Education, the Edmonton Public Schools, and the York Region Roman Catholic School System) employ any first language assessment procedures is an indication of how low a priority non-discriminatory assessment is for Canadian policy-makers.

Conclusion

Currently our global community is characterized by increasing cross-national contact as a result of technological and economic development (e.g. electronic media, ease of travel, mobility of labour, etc). Internally, in most of the western countries, cultural and linguistic diversity is continuing to increase dramatically. In Canada, for example, very significant increases in immigration are forecast during the next 20 years, and this will lead to further diversity in our schools and society. Thus, the issue is not whether linguistic and cultural diversity are desirable or not; they are an inevitable reality.

The issue is rather whether our energies as a nation are better spent denying our emerging multilingual and multicultural identity or accepting the linguistic assets that minorities bring to Canada and promoting them as we would any other human resource. Despite our racist history and current manifestations of intolerance and discrimination, Canadian policies towards minorities are among the more enlightened in the western world. Yet far more could be done if we were to substitute imagination for pettiness by establishing alternative schools or programs where all Canadian students would have the opportunity to develop literacy and fluency in at least three languages. We have abundant research knowledge upon which to base such schools at the present time. We simply choose not to enrich our children.

A major reason why we make this seemingly absurd choice is that to implement such trilingual schools would amount to an explicit valorization of multilingualism and an elevation of the status of minority groups whose languages would now be institutionalized within the mainstream educational system. In other words, such initiatives would alter the power relations between dominant and subordinate groups within Canadian society. Our refusal to develop a linguistically-competent society is rationalized on financial, administrative, and educational grounds but the simple fact is that the dominant groups in Canadian society have little interest in institutionalizing the languages of the "other ethnic groups," no matter what long-term benefits may accrue to Canada as a result of becoming more linguistically competent. It remains to be seen whether changing international realities will alter this pattern.

REFERENCES

Abella, I. & Troper, H. (1982)
— *None is too many.*, Toronto: Lester and Orpen Dennys.

Ada, A.F. (1988)
— "The Pajaro Valley experience: Working with Spanish-speaking parents to develop children's reading and writing skills in the home through the use of children's literature." In T. Skutnabb-Kangas & J. Cummins (Eds.) *Minority education: From shame to struggle.* Clevedon, England: Multilingual

Ahlgren, I. (1982)
— *Sign language and the learning of Swedish by deaf children.* Newsletter School Research, 2. Stockholm: National Board of Education.

Amiel-Eleftheriadou, N-O. (1989)
— *The case of Greek-Canadian students: Some factors affecting their positive or negative attitude towards their mother-tongue.* Unpublished paper, Ontario Institute for Studies in Education.

Anderson, J.T.M. (1918)
— *The education of the New Canadian.* Toronto: Dent.

Ashworth, M. (1988)
— *Blessed with Bilingual Brains: Education of immigrant children with English as a second language.* Vancouver: Pacific Educational Press.

Baetens Beardsmore, H. & Kohls, J. (1988)
— "Immediate pertinence in the acquisition of multilingual proficiency: The European schools." *Canadian Modern Language Review*, 44, 680-701.

Baetens Beardsmore, H.& Lebrun, N. (in press)
— "Trilingual education in the Grand Duchy of Luxembourg." To appear in *Focusschriften in Honour of Joshua Fishman.* Amsterdam & New York: Benjamins, 1990.

Baker, C. & Battison, R. (1980)
— *Sign language and the Deaf community.* Washington, D.C.: National Association for the Deaf.

Barber, J. (1988)
— "School board jungle." *Toronto, Globe and Mail*, February, 28-53.

Berry, J.W., Kalin, R.& Taylor, D.M. (1977)
— *Multiculturalism and ethnic attitudes in Canada.* Ottawa: Ministry of Supply and Services Canada.

Berryman, J. (1986)
— *Implementation of Ontario's Heritage Languages Program: A case study of the extended school day model.* Unpublished doctoral dissertation, University of Toronto.

Bhatnagar, J. (1980)
— *Linguistic behaviour and adjustment of immigrant children in French and English schools in Montreal.* International Review of Applied

Psychology, 29, 141-159.

Black, N.F. (1913)
— *English for the Non-English*. Regina: Regina Book Shop Limited.

Bureau des Services aux Communautés Culturelles (1983)
— *Programme d'Enseignement des Langues d'Origine (P.E.L.O.): Etat de la situation*. Québec: Gouvernement du Québec.

Canadian Ethnocultual Council (1988)
— *The other Canadian languages: A report on the status of heritage languages across Canada*. Ottawa: Canadian Ethnocultural Council.

Carey, S. & Cummins, J. (1979)
— *English and French achievement of grade 5 children from English, French, and mixed French-English home backgrounds attending the Edmonton Separate School System English-French immersion program*. Report submitted to the Edmonton Separate School System.

Chapman, E. (1981)
— *An evaluation of the first two years of the English-Ukrainian bilingual program: Summary report*. Winnipeg: Manitoba Department of Education.

Collenette, D.M. (1984)
— *The place of multiculturalism in Canada's long-tern economic development*. A brief submitted to the Royal Commission on the Economic Union and Development Prospects for Canada. March.

Comité d'Implantation du Plan d'Action à l'Intention des Communautés Culturelles, (1983)
— *Rapport annuel 1981-1982*. Québec: Editeur Officiel du Québec.

Commissioner of Official Languages. (1983)
— *Annual Report, 1983*. Ottawa: Commissioner of Official Languages.

Conseil Superieur de l'Education. (1983)
— *L'Education interculturelle: Avis au ministre de l'éducation*. Québec: Gouvernement du Québec.

Coxe, D. (1985)
— "The back page: Occidental to a fault: The languages most important to our commercial future are the ones we study the least." *Canadian Business*, February.

Cummins, J. (1981)
— *Effects of kindergarten experience on academic progress in French immersion programs*. Toronto: Ontario Ministry of Education.

Cummins, J. (1983)
— *Heritage language education: A literature review*. Toronto: Ministry of Education, Ontario.

Cummins, J. (1984)
— *Bilingualism and special education: Issues in assessment and pedagogy*. Clevedon, England: Multilingual Matters.

Cummins, J. (1988)
— "From multicultural to anti-racist education: An analysis of programmes and policies in Ontario." In T. Skutnabb-Kangas and J. Cummins (eds.) *Minority education: From shame to struggle*. Clevedon, England:

Multilingual Matters.

Cummins, J. (1989)
— *Empowering minority students*. Sacramento: California Association for Bilingual Education.

Cummins, J. & Mulcahy, R. (1978)
— "Orientation to language in Ukrainian-English bilingual children." *Child Development*, 49, 1239-1242.

Cummins, J. & Troper, H. (1985)
— "Multiculturalism and language policy in Canada." In J. Cobarrubias (ed.) *Language policy in Canada: Current issues*. Quebec: CIRB/ICRB.

Cummins, J., Ramos, J. & Lopes, J. (1989)
— *The transition from home to school: A longitudinal study of Portuguese-speaking children*. Unpublished research report, OISE.

Cziko, G. (1975)1975.
— *The effects of different French immersion programs on the language and academic skills of children from various socioeconomic backgrounds*. M.A. Thesis, Department of Psychology, McGill University.

Danesi, M. (1986)
— *Teaching a language to children from dialect backgrounds*. Toronto: OISE Press.

Danesi, M. (1988)
— *Studies in heritage language learning and teaching*. Toronto: Centro Canadese Sculola e Cultura Italiana.

Danesi, M., Cicogna, C., Menechella, G. & Gaspari, A. (in press)
— *La correlazione tra studio della lingua madre e lo sviluppo della lingua dominante*. Rassegna Italiana di Linguistica Applicata.

Danesi, M. & DiGiovanni, A. (1989)
— "Italian as a heritage language in Ontario: A historical sketch." *Polyphony*, 11, 89-94.

Davis, B.K. (1987)
— *An analysis of the public responses to the Proposal for Action: Ontario's Heritage Languages Program*. Toronto: Ministry of Education, Ontario.

Delgado, G.L. (1984)
— "Hearing-Impaired children from non-native-language homes." In G.L. Delgado (Ed.) *The Hispanic Deaf: Issues and challenges for bilingual special education*. Washington, D.C.: Gallaudet College Press.

Deosaran, R. & Gershman, J.S. (1976)
— *An evaluation of the 1975-76 Chinese-Canadian bi-cultural program*. Toronto: Toronto Board of Education, Research Report #137.

Dolson, D. (1985)
— "The effects of Spanish home language use on the scholastic performance of Hispanic pupils." *Journal of Multilingual and Multicultural Development*, 6, 135-156.

d'Onofrio, M. (1988)
— *A descriptive study of bilingualism and biliteracy development in two pre-school Italo-Canadian children*. Unpublished doctoral dissertation,

University of Toronto.

Edmonton Public Schools. (1980)
— *Summary of the evaluations of the bilingual English-Ukrainian and bilingual English-French program*. Edmonton: Edmonton Public School Board.

Edwards, H.P. & Casserly, M.P. (1973)
— *Evaluation of second language programs in the English schools*. Annual report, Ottawa Roman Catholic Separate School Board.

Egyed, C. (1973)
— *The attainment of English language skills as a function of instruction in the native tongue of Italian kindergarten children*. Paper presented to the Canadian Psychological Association conference, Victoria, June.

Elwood, W. (1989)
— "Learning by root." *New Internationalist*, January.

Ewanyshyn, E. (1979)
— *Evaluation of a Ukrainian-English bilingual program, 1978-79*. Edmonton: Edmonton Catholic Schools.

Ewanyshyn, E. (1980)
— *Evaluation of a Ukrainian-English bilingual program, 1978-79*. Edmonton: Edmonton Catholic Schools.

European Commission. (1978)
— *Activities for the education and vocational training of migrant workers and their families in the European Community*. Contribution to the Standing Conference of European Ministers of Education.

Ewoldt, C. (1987)
— "Reading tests and the deaf reader. Can we measure how well deaf students read?" *Perspectives for Teachers of the Hearing Impaired*, 5, 21-24.

Feuerstein, R. (1979)
— *The dynamic assessment of retarded performers: The learning potential assessment device*. Baltimore: University Park Press.

Feuerverger, G. (1982)
— *Effects of the heritage language program on the ethnolinguistic vitality of Italo-Canadian students*. Unpublished M.A. Thesis, Ontario Institute for Studies in Education.

Fox, J., Coles, M., Haddon, S., & Munns, R. (1987)
— *Study visit to Toronto. Multi-Cultural education*. Unpublished report.

French, O. (1989)
— "Conway assailed for failing to make changes in deaf education." *The Globe and Mail*, December 21, A16.

Genesee, F. (1976)
— "The suitability of immersion programs for all children." *Canadian Modern Language Review*, 32, 494-515.

Genesee, F. & Lambert, W.E. (1980)
— *Trilingual education for the majority group child*. Unpublished research report, McGill University.

Genesee, F., Tucker, G.R. & Lambert, W.E. (1978a)
— "An experiment in trilingual education: Report 3". *Canadian Modern Language Review*, 34, 621-643.

Genesee, F., Tucker, G.R. & Lambert, W.E. (1978b)
— "An experiment in trilingual education: Report 4." *Language Learning*. 28, 343-365.

Giroux, H. (1988)
— *Teachers as intellectuals: Toward a critical pedagogy of learning*. Granby, MA: Bergin & Garvey.

Gouvernement du Québec. (1981)
— *Autant de façons d'être québécois: Plan d'action du gouvernement du Québec à l'intention des communautés culturelles*. (English version: Quebeckers each and every one), Québec: Gouvernement du Québec.

Government of Alberta. (1988)
— *Language education policy for Alberta*. Edmonton: Government of Alberta.

Grande, A. (1975)
— "A transition program for young immigrant children." In A. Wolfgang (ed.) *Education of immigrant students: Issues and answers*. Toronto: OISE.

Hansen, B. (1987)
— "Sign language and bilingualism: A focus on an experimental approach to the teaching of deaf children in Denmark." In J. Kyle (Ed.) *Sign in School*. Clevedon, England: Multilingual Matters.

Harney, R. & Troper, H. (1975)
— *Immigrants: A portrait of urban experience 1890-1930*. Toronto: Van Nostrand Rheinhold.

Hébert, R. et al. (1976)
— *Rendement académique et langue d'enseignement chez les élèves franco-manitobains*. Saint-Boniface, Manitoba: Centre de Recherches du Collège Universitaire de Saint-Boniface.

Henderson, K. (1977)
— *A report on bilingual transition programs for Italian and Portuguese immigrant students*. Unpublished research report, Ontario Institute for Studies in Education.

Hunt, K. (1970)
— *Syntactic maturity in school children and adults*. Monographs of the Society for Research in Child Development, 35, (whole no. 134).

Israelite, N., Ewoldt, C., Hoffmeister, R. et al. (1989)
— *A review of the literature on the effective use of native sign language on the acquisition of a majority language by hearing impaired students*. Research Project N. 1170. Final Report to the Ontario Ministry of Education, October.

Johnson, W. (1982)
— "Creating a nation of tongues." *Globe and Mail*, June 26.

Jones, J. (1984)
— "Multilingual approach reflects Canadian mosaic." *Language and*

Society, No. 12, p. 33-38.

Kalantzis, M., Cope, B., & Slade, D. (1989)
— *Minority languages and dominant culture: Issues of education, assessment and social equity*. Barcombe, England: The Falmer Press.

Kalantzis, M., Cope, B., Noble, G., & Poynting, S. (1989)
— *Cultures of schooling: Pedagogies for cultural difference and social access*. Wollongong: Centre for Multicultural Studies.

Keyser, R. & Brown, J. (1981)
— *Heritage language program survey*. Unpublished research report, Metropolitan Separate School Board.

Krashen, S.D. & Biber, D. (1988)
— *On course: Bilingual education's success in California*. Sacramento: California Association for Bilingual Education.

Lado, R., Hanson, I., & D'Emilio, T. (1980)
— "Biliteracy for bilingual children by grade 1: The SED Center Preschool Reading Project." In J.A. Alatis (ed.) *Current issues in bilingual education*. Washington, DC: Georgetown University Press.

Lambert, W. (1990)
— "Persistent issues in bilingualism." In Harley, B., Allen, P., Cummins, J., & Swain, M. *The development of second language proficiency*. Cambridge: Cambridge University Press.

Lane, H. (1984)
— *When the mind hears: A history of the Deaf*. New York: Vintage Books.

Lane, H. (1988)
— "Is there a "Psychology of the Deaf"?" *Exceptional Children*, 55, 7-19.

Lapkin, S. & Swain, M. (1977)
— "The use of English and French cloze tests in a bilingual education program evaluation: Validity and error analysis." *Language Learning*, 27, 279-313.

Larter, S. & Cheng, D. (1986)
— *Teaching heritage languages and cultures in an integrated/extended day*. Research Report #181. Toronto: Toronto Board of Education.

Lerman, A. (1976)
— *Discovering and meeting the needs of Hispanic hearing impaired children*. (Final Report CREED VII Project). New York: Lexington School for the Deaf.

Lind, L. (1974)
— *The learning machine: A hard look at Toronto schools*. Toronto: Anansi.

Livingstone, D.W. & Hart, D.J. (1983)
— *Public attitudes toward education in Ontario 1982: fourth OISE Survey*. Toronto: OISE.

Lo Bianco, J. (1987)
— *National policy on languages*. Canberra: Australian government Publishing Service.

Lo Bianco, J. (1989)
— *Revitalizing multicultural education in Australia*. Multiculturalism, 12,

30-39.

Lupul, M. (1976)
— "Bilingual education and the Ukrainians in Western Canada: Possibilities and problems." In M. Swain (ed.) *Bilingualism in Canadian education: Issues and research.* Edmonton: Canadian Society for the Study of Education.

Lupul, M. (1981)
— *The political implementation of multiculturalism.* Paper presented to the Ninth Biennial Conference of the Canadian Ethnic Studies Association.

MacCormack, R. (1989)
— "This playgroup looks the same but sounds different." *The Forerunner*, 2, Autumn, 12-13.

MacNamee, T. & White, H. (1985)
— "Heritage language in the preschool." *Language and Society*, No. 15, Winter, 20-23.

Malarek, V. (1989)
— "Quebec grapples with how to maintain French-speaking majority". *Globe and Mail*, October 30.

Mallea, J.R. (1989)
— *Schooling in a plural Canada.* Clevedon, England: Multilingual Matters.

Masemann, V.L. (1978-79)
— "Multicultural programs in Toronto schools." *Interchange*, 9, 29-44.

Masemann, V. & Cummins, J. (1985)
— *Education: Cultural and linguistic pluralism in Canada.* Ottawa: Multiculturalism Canada.

Memmi, A. (1966)
— *Portrait du colonisé.* Paris: Pauvert.

McFadyen, J. (1983)
— "System overload." *Role Call*, 6, p. 2.

Ministry of Education, Ontario (s.d.)
— *Ontario's heritage language program.* Information pamphlet.

Ministry of Education, Ontario(1987)
— *Proposal for Action: Ontario's Heritage Languages Program.* Toronto: Ministry of Education.

Moody J.L. (1974)
— *Evaluation of the Punjabi-English class at the Moberly Primary Annex for the 1973-74 school year.* Research report 74-18. Vancouver: Vancouver Board of School Trustees, Department of Planning and Evaluation.

Musselman, C., Lindsay, P., & Wilson, A. (1988)
— "The effect of mothers' communication mode on language development in preschool deaf children." *Applied Psycholinguistics*, 9, 185-204.

O'Bryan, K.G., Reitz, J.& Kuplowska, O. (1976)
— *Non-official languages.* Ottawa: Supply and Services Canada.

Ogbu, J. (1978)
— *Minority education and caste.* New York: Academic Press.

Picard, A. (1989)
— "School board survey irks Montreal groups." *Globe and Mail*, November 9.

Popp, L.A. (1976)
— "The English competence of French-speaking students in a bilingual setting." *Canadian Modern Language Review*, 32, 365-377.

Ramphal, D.K. (1983)
— *An analysis of reading instruction of West Indian Creole-speaking students.* Unpublished doctoral dissertation, The Ontario Institute for Studies in Education.

Ramphal, D.K. (1984)
— "The effects of culture on black children's reading." *Multiculturalism*, 7, 22-27.

Report of the Special Committee on Visible Minorities in Canadian Society. (1984)
— *Equality now!* Ottawa: House of Commons.

Rocher, G. (1973)
— *Le Québec en mutation.* Montreal: Hurtubise.

Royal Commission on Bilingualism and Biculturalism (1966)
— *Preliminary report.* Ottawa: Ministry of Supply and Services Canada.

Royal Commission on Bilingualism and Biculturalism (1970)
— *Book IV. The cultural contribution of the other ethnic groups.* Ottawa: Ministry of Supply and Services Canada.

Rudser, S.F. (1988)
— "Sign language instruction and its implication for the deaf." In M. Strong (Ed.) *Language learning and deafness.* New York: Cambridge University Press.

Ryan, W. (1976)
— *Blaming the victim.* New York: Vintage Books.

Saif, P. & Sheldon, M. (1969)
— *An investigation of the experimental French programme at Bedford Park and Allenby Public Schools.* Research report, Toronto Board of Education.

Samuda, R.J. & Crawford, D.H. (1980)
— *Testing, assessment, counselling and placement of ethnic minority students.* Toronto: Ministry of Education, Ontario.

Samuda, R.J., Kong, S.L., Cummins, J., Lewis, J.& Pascual-Leone, J. (1989)
— *Assessment and placement of minority students.* Toronto: C.J. Hogrefe and ISSP.

Saskatchewan Organization for Heritage Languages (s.d.)
— *Heritage languages can bring the world to you.* Regina: SOHL.

Scarino, A., Vale, D., McKay, P.,& Clark, J. (1988)
— *Australian language levels guidelines: Book 1. Language learning in Australia. Book 2. Syllabus development and programming. Book 3. Method, Resources, and Assessment. Book 4. Evaluation, curriculum renewal, and teacher development.* Woden, A.C.T.: Curriculum Development Centre.

Shapson, S. & Purbhoo, M. (1977)
— "A transition program for Italian children." *Canadian Modern Language Journal*, 33, p. 486-496.

Shaw, J. (1983)
— "Gaelic revisited: Maintaining Gaelic in Cape Breton in the '80s." In J. Cummins (Ed.) *Heritage language education: Issues and directions*. Ottawa: Multiculturalism Canada.

Sissons, C.B. (1917)
— *Bi-lingual schools in Canada*. Dent: London.

Skutnabb-Kangas, T. (1984)
— *Bilingualism or not: The education of minorities*. Clevedon, England: Multilingual Matters.

Skutnabb-Kangas, T. & Cummins, J. (1988)
— *Minority education: From shame to struggle*. Clevedon, England: Multilingual Matters.

Snow, C.E. & Hakuta, K.
— *The costs of monolingualism*. Santa Cruz: Bilingual Research Group University of California Santa Cruz.

Swain, M. & Lapkin, S. (1982)
— *Evaluating bilingual education*. Clevedon, England: Multilingual Matters.

Swain, M. Lapkin, S., Rowen, N., & Hart, D. (1988)
— *The role of mother tongue literacy in third language learning*. Paper presented at the SSHRC Conference on Exploring the Breadth and Depth of Literacy, St. John's Newfoundland, September.

Swisher, M.V. (1984)
— "Signed input of hearing mothers to deaf children." *Language Learning,* 34, 69-86.

Task Force on Multiculturalism (1989)
— *Multiculturalism in Saskatchewan*. Report to Ministers' Committee on Multiculturalism. Saskatchewan Parks, Recreation and Culture.

Titone, R. (1988)
— "From cognitive to integrated models of second language acquisition." In V.S. Lee (ed.) *Language teaching and learning: Canada and Italy*. Ottawa: Canadian Academic Centre in Italy.

Toronto Board of Education (1975)
— *Draft report of the Work Group on Multicultural Programs*. Toronto: Toronto Board of Education.

Toronto Board of Education. (1976
— *Final report of the Work Group on Multicultural Programs*. Toronto: Toronto Board of Education.

Toronto Board of Education (1982)
— *Towards a comprehensive language policy. The final report of the Work Group on Third Language Instruction*. Toronto: Toronto Board of Education.

Troike, R. (1978)
— "Research evidence for the effectiveness of bilingual education". *NABE*

Journal, 3, 13-24.

Troper, H. (1979)
— "An uncertain past: Reflections on the history of multiculturalism." *TESL Talk*, 10, 7-15.

Ukrainian Canadian Committee School Board (1987)
— *Suggestions for "Proposal for Action: Ontario's Heritage Languages Program."* Brief submitted by the Ukrainian Canadian Committee School Board to the Ontario Ministry of Education.

Valli, C., Thumann-Prezioso, C., Lucas, C., Liddell, S.K.,& Johnson, R.E. (1989)
— *An open letter to the campus community.* Gallaudet College.

Valpy, M. (1989)
— "Canadians' charity was always a myth." *Globe and Mail*, March 21.

Watson, J. (1988)
— *Gaelic language teaching in Cape Breton.* Paper presented at the National Conference on Heritage Language Teacher Training, OISE, Toronto, 1988.

Weiner, G. (1989)
— *Speaking notes for the Honourable Gerry Weiner, Secretary of State of Canada and Minister of State Multiculturalism and Citizenship.* March 21, International Day for the Elimination of Racial Discrimination.

Wells, G. (1981)
— *Learning through interaction: The study of language development.* Cambridge: Cambridge University Press.

Wechsler, D. (1974)
— *WISC-R Manual.* New York: Psychological Corporation.

Wilson, A.K. (1983)
— *A consumer's guide to Bill 82: Special education in Ontario.* Toronto: O.I.S.E.

Wright, E.N. & Tsuji, G.K. (1984)
— *The grade nine student survey: Fall 1983.* Toronto: Toronto Board of Education, Research Report No. 174.

Wynnyckyj, O. (1989a)
— "Why no bilingual education in Ontario?" *New Perspectives,* February.

Wynnyckyj, O. (1989b)
— "Language is political." *New Perspectives*, June.

APPENDIX

EDUCATIONAL EFFECTS OF HERITAGE LANGUAGE PROGRAMS[1]

A. Enrichment Programs Designed to Promote Bilingualism

1. English-Ukrainian (Edmonton Public School Board.)

In September 1973, the Edmonton Public School Board (EPSB) introduced the English-Ukrainian bilingual program at the Kindergarten level. In Kindergarten 100% of the instructional time was in Ukrainian, after which instructional time was divided equally between English and Ukrainian. Mathematics, English language arts, and science were taught in English, while social studies, physical education, Ukrainian language arts, art, and music were taught in Ukrainian.

More than three-quarters of the students came from homes in which one or both parents could speak Ukrainian and only about 10% of the students had no Ukrainian ancestry. However, only about 15% of the students were fluent in Ukrainian on entry to school. Unlike typical students in French immersion programs, the bilingual students were representative of the EPSB system in terms of both ability level and parental socioeconomic status. For example, their Grade 1 score (averaged over five years from 1974 to 1978) on the Metropolitan Readiness Test was only one point above the EPSB mean, and less than 50% of the parents had post-secondary education (Edmonton Public Schools, 1980).

In the first year of the evaluation, control students were chosen from among students in regular unilingual English program classes across the EPSB system whose parents had the same socioeconomic level and knowledge of Ukrainian as the program parents. In subsequent years control students were randomly chosen from the same schools as students in the bilingual program. The selection was stratified on the basis of gender, school, and ability level.

No consistent pattern of differences emerged in comparisons of English and mathematics skills between program and control students in the early grades. However, at the Grade 5 level (the last year of the evaluation) the first cohort of bilingual program students performed significantly better than control students in mathematics and on both decoding and comprehension subtests of the standardized reading test that was administered.

The evaluation carried out by the EPSB also examined the issue of whether the program was equally appropriate for students of different ability levels. This was done by dividing students into high, medium and low ability levels and testing for program-by-ability interaction effects in a two-way analysis of variance design. No evidence of interaction effects was found, indicating that low-ability students had no more difficulty in the bilingual program than they would have had in the regular program.

A study was carried out with Grade 1 and 3 students in order to investigate bilingual children's metalinguistic development. The study (Cummins and Mulcahy, 1978) revealed that students who were relatively fluent in Ukrainian because their parents used it consistently at home were significantly better able to detect ambiguities in English sentence structure than either equivalent unilingual English-speaking children not in the program or children in the program who came from predominantly English-speaking homes.

The EPSB evaluation also reported that students' Ukrainian skills developed in accord with program expectations, and they also developed an appreciation for and knowledge about the Ukrainian culture. In addition, a large majority of the parents and program personnel were pleased with the program, felt the students were happy, and wished the program to be continued to higher grade levels.

2. English-Ukrainian (Edmonton Catholic School Board)

The Edmonton Catholic School Board's (ECSB) bilingual program was instituted at the same time as the EPSB program. The program itself was similar to that in the EPSB with the exception that religious instruction in the Ukrainian Catholic Rite was carried out in the ECSB program but not in the EPSB.

As the program progressed through the grades, students were matched with comparison students from the same schools on the basis of grade, socioeconomic status, gender, age and Primary Mental Ability score, and the performance of matched groups on a variety of achievement tests was compared. The 1977/78 and 1978/79 evaluations (Ewanyshyn, 1979, 1980) will be considered here since they involve comparisons of students between Grades 1 and 5. Approximately 380 students were involved in the evaluation in each of these years.

The comparisons indicated that students in the bilingual program progressed academically at least as well as students in the regular English-only program. The 1977/78 evaluation reported seven significant group differences in achievement (in English), six of which favoured the bilingual program. The most frequent group differences in achievement were on measures of reading comprehension and spelling. In addition, parents, teachers, and principals all showed high levels of satisfaction with the program.

3. English-Ukrainian (Manitoba)

In September 1979, an English-Ukrainian bilingual program was implemented in one Grade 1 class in each of three school divisions in Manitoba. In subsequent years the program spread rapidly to other school divisions, with Kindergarten as the starting grade. The program was based on the Edmonton model and the evaluation was conducted by the Manitoba Department of Education (Chapman, 1981).

The evaluation of the first two years of the program involved 262 program students in Kindergarten and Grades 1 and 2. The scores of these students were compared with those of regular program students in the same schools. Comparison of the Metropolitan Readiness Test scores of Kindergarten students who subsequently entered either the bilingual or regular Grade 1 program showed no significant differences, suggesting that students in the bilingual program are representative of the general school population.

Eighty-eight percent of the parental respondents (N=203) reported that their child was of Ukrainian descent. Ukrainian was spoken at least half the time in 23% of the respondents' homes, while 76% of the respondents' children regularly interacted with Ukrainian-speaking people. Thus, the students in the Manitoba program appear very similar in background to students in the Edmonton programs.

Comparison of students who attended regular and Ukrainian Kindergartens revealed no differences in English "readiness" skills, despite the fact that the Ukrainian Kindergarten was conducted for about 70% of the time in Ukrainian. No differences in English or other subject matter achievement were found between program and comparison students at either the Grade 1 or 2 levels, despite the fact that the comparison groups had spent about twice as much time being taught in English. Teachers, principals, and parents all expressed a high degree of satisfaction with the program.

B. Enrichment Programs Designed to Promote Trilingualism

1. The Montreal Hebrew-English Programs

Trilingual or bilingual programs involving Hebrew exist in most of the major Canadian cities and are usually, but not always, operated outside of the regular public school system. Other isolated examples of trilingual education exist; for example, in one predominantly Italian-background school in the Toronto Metropolitan Separate School Board (St. Gaspar), students from Grades 5 to 8 are enrolled in the board's French-English bilingual program (starting in grade 5) and also take Italian for half-an-hour a day during regular school hours (Feuerverger, 1982). However, only the Montreal trilingual programs have been systematically evaluated.

Because the program variations compared by Genesee Tucker and Lambert (1978a, 1978b) are complex, only the general pattern of findings is reported here. The basic design involved comparing groups of students who participated in two slightly different "early double immersion" (EDI) programs (i.e. Hebrew-French-English trilingual programs) with students who attended a more traditional Hebrew day school (most initial instruction through the medium of English and Hebrew, but with increasing amounts of French-medium instruction in the intermediate grades of elementary school). The Hebrew time allocation and curriculum was similar in all three schools. In one of the EDI schools, English language arts was introduced in Grade 3, and in Grade 4 in the other school. The academic performance of students in these schools was also compared with that of students in regular French immersion and core French-as-a-second-language programs.

It was found that at the Grades 4 and 5 levels both EDI groups achieved as well in English as all other groups, despite considerably less time spent in English-medium instruction than the traditional Hebrew day school or core French-as-a-second-language groups. No group differences were evident in mathematics, despite the fact that the EDI groups had received all initial math instruction in French, whereas the traditional Hebrew day school students received all initial math instruction in English. The EDI students scored almost as well as the regular French immersion students on measures of French proficiency. On measures of Hebrew, the EDI students tended to score higher than students in the regular Hebrew day school despite the similarity of program and time allocation.

Genesee and Lambert (1980) conclude that programs of bi- and trilingualism are feasible and effective ways of enriching students' elementary education insofar as

> The Hebrew day schools were able (1) to achieve the goals of regular school programs with regard to native language development and academic achievement, (2) to maintain important religious, cultural and linguistic traditions, and (3) at the same time, to develop the children's competence in a language of local importance. (p. 25)

The authors acknowledge that the students in the trilingual programs were highly capable and motivated youngsters, but point out that the existing evidence (e.g. Cziko, 1975) pertaining to the suitability of single French immersion programs for students who are less economically and intellectually advantaged suggests that these students would also benefit academically and linguistically from programs of double immersion.

C. Transitional Bilingual Programs

1. Italian Kindergarten Transition Program in Toronto (Shapson & Purbhoo, 1977)

In the early 1970s the Toronto Board of Education implemented an experimental transition program which allowed the curriculum to be presented in the child's first language (Italian) during the two introductory Kindergarten years of schooling (i.e. ages 4-5, 5-6). The original proposal (Grande, 1975) had recommended that literacy skills be introduced in the child's first language but this was rejected by the board because the Ontario Education Act prohibited the use of languages other than English or French as a medium of instruction except on a temporary basis to ease students' integration into the school system. Because of this legal restriction, promotion of Italian skills was not an objective of the program.

Almost all students in the program were born in Canada and had learned Italian (or dialect) as a first language. Seventy-nine percent of the parents spoke Italian extensively with their children, but only 53% of the children still spoke Italian as the main language at home. Only seven percent of children who had older siblings were spoken to in Italian by these siblings. Thus, at the start of the program some children used more English than Italian, whereas others spoke no English at all.

In the classroom standard Italian, dialect, and English were all used quite freely with frequent spontaneous switching of languages by students and teacher. The proportion of English use increased consistently during the Junior Kindergarten (JK) year and by the Senior Kindergarten (SK) year "Italian was used only occasionally in activities involving the whole class, but more often with a few individuals who still used their mother tongue" (Shapson and Purbhoo, 1977, p. 489).

The evaluation of the transition program involved observations of verbal participation in the classroom, tests of language comprehension, teacher assessments of student progress, and parent questionnaires. Comparisons were made with students in regular kindergarten classes from two other schools whose students had language backgrounds similar to those of the program students. There is little reason to suspect initial pre-treatment differences between program and comparison students since virtually all parents who were offered the transition option in the program school accepted it and the enrolment justified two transition classes.

Classroom observations showed that a significantly larger proportion of students in the transition classes participated in class discussions (59% v. 43%), and contributed both spontaneously (45% v. 28%) and in response to questions (41% v. 28%). Shapson and Purbhoo suggest that

> Increased participation in class discussions may be considered
> a signal that the child feels comfortable and important in school.
> It might be viewed as an indicator of self-concept. (p. 490)

No group differences in English (or Italian) language comprehension as measured by the Peabody Picture Vocabulary Test were found in either JK or SK. Teachers' ratings of overall academic performance revealed more positive comments for the transition students in SK. Shapson and Purbhoo caution, however, that this result may be due to differences in teachers' styles of reporting.

It was also reported that "while parents from the comparison group expressed as great an interest in their children's education, the transition group parents attended more school functions, participated more in classroom events and talked regularly with the teacher" (1977, p. 493). Shapson and Purbhoo attribute this greater involvement to the obvious fact that a common language makes communication easier.

In summary, the program objectives were clearly met in that participation by students and their parents in the educational process was facilitated by the incorporation of Italian as a medium of instruction.

2. English-Italian Kindergarten Program in Ottawa (Egyed, 1973)

Egyed (1973) compared the academic progress in SK of three groups of Italian-background students randomly assigned to (1) a full-day English Kindergarten, (2) a half-day English, half-day Italian Kindergarten, and (3) a half-day English, half-day French Kindergarten. Using a pre- and post-test design, Egyed reported no significant differences in English academic progress between students in the bilingual Italian-English program compared to those in the full-day English program. Thus, using Italian as the medium of instruction for half the school day did not interfere with students' progress in English.

However, Italian-background students in the French-English bilingual Kindergarten program obtained significantly lower scores in English academic skills than students in either of the two other programs. The French-English bilingual students were reported to have made "relatively low gains in auditory psycho-linguistic development" (Edwards and Casserly, 1973, p. 248).

In summary, this study is consistent with the others reviewed in showing that instructional time spent through the medium of minority children's mother tongue entails no academic cost to their progress in English.

3. Vancouver Punjabi-English Transition Program (Moody, 1974)

This program was intended to assist newly-arrived 5- to 8-year-old immigrant children from the Punjab to learn English and integrate into the regular program. The teacher used both Punjabi and English for instructional purposes. In general, the program appears to have effectively met its objectives of promoting both language and self-concept development in that the experimental students made at least as rapid progress as comparison East Indian students. By the end of the first year of the program, more than half the students were judged to have made sufficient progress in English to merit placement in the regular English program.

4. Toronto Italian and Portuguese Transition Programs (Henderson, 1977)

These experimental programs were developed in the Metropolitan Separate School Board (MSSB) for children in grades 4, 5, and 6 who came directly from Italian- and Portuguese-speaking countries. A bilingual teacher maintained an academic program in students' first language over the course of one year while English was being acquired. The evaluation design for Italian and Portuguese programs differed somewhat and thus each will be considered separately.

Italian Program Results

The Italian class was begun in September 1973 with 15 recently-arrived students who could read and write in Italian. The control sample was selected from comparable students who had been in an ESL program the previous year and had immigrated to Toronto approximately one year earlier. The control group was post-tested with the Metropolitan Achievement Test (MAT) in October 1973 and the experimental group was tested in October 1974. Parents of both groups were also interviewed. The lack of a pretest and the small number of students clearly warrant caution in interpreting the results, although there appears to be no obvious reason why the two groups would differ in initial characteristics.

No statistically significant differences were found on the MAT, but differences of about one half year in grade-equivalents were found in favour of the control group in spelling and in favour of the experimental group in math concepts and problem solving. Henderson (1977) points out that

> Selection of the control students biased the results against the experimental program since at the time of testing, the control students had been in Canada approximately eight months longer than the students of the experimental program (a difference of 22 to 14 months on the average). (p. 4)

The parent interviews revealed that although both sets of parents claimed that they contacted the school equally often, two-thirds of the experimental group knew the name of their children's teacher, while none of the control group were able to identify the teacher by name. Henderson (1977) summarizes the parent interview data as follows:

> ...parents of experimental students reported that their children spoke more Italian around home and had higher academic aspirations which were also more consistent with those of the parents themselves. Parents with children in the experimental program had more specific knowledge of the school and its personnel. (p. 5)

These results are generally similar to those of other transition programs in suggesting satisfactory academic progress and greater parental involvement than in regular English programs.

Portuguese Program Results

The Portuguese evaluation involved a larger number of students (two experimental classes) and had a tighter research design than the Italian study. The program was begun in September 1974 in two schools in the same general area. Control students were drawn from three classes in two other schools in the same area.

A Portuguese translation/adaptation of the MAT was used as a pre-test and the English version was given as the post-test. An analysis of covariance design was used to help control for any pre-test differences. Significant post-test differences in favour of the experimental group were observed on three subtests of the MAT, namely, language, math concepts, and problem solving. Although not statistically significant, differences favoured the experimental group on three of the other four subtests, and in some cases (including spelling) by the equivalent of nearly half a year of progress.

Students' oral English was also assessed by means of a picture description task. Both groups produced approximately the same number of sentences, but the sentences of the experimental group averaged significantly more words. Words-per-sentence (or "T-unit") is often used as an index of linguistic complexity (Hunt, 1970).

Verbal interactions in the experimental and control classes were observed in the early spring of the school year. It was found that in the experimental classes Portuguese was used by the teachers to support explanations and instructions as well as in informal student-student and teacher-student conversation. In the control classes, only English was used in teacher-student exchanges and students were less likely to use Portuguese in informal conversation.

Conclusion

Virtually all the evaluations reviewed, whether of enrichment or transition programs, show clearly that time spent with the minority language as the medium of instruction results in no academic loss to students' progress in the majority language. In some cases, in fact, students who received less English instruction performed significantly better in English academic skills than comparison groups in all-English programs.

FOOTNOTES

[1] This review of evaluation studies is based on Chapter 2 of J. Cummins' "Heritage Language Education: A Literature Review" (Toronto: Ministry of Education, 1983).

Join the Debate
On What Should Happen In
Canada's Schools

The issues raised in books like this one will be carried on the pages of *Our Schools / Our Selves: a magazine for Canadian education activists.*

The best way to keep in touch is to fill out the postage-paid subscription form at the back of this book and mail it in.

But we hope you'll do more than read us. We hope you'll get involved in these issues, if you aren't already. And that you'll let us know what you think of our books and articles.

For a year's subscription you'll get 4 magazines and 4 books.

The next issue of the magazine (March 1990) will include articles on:

◆ **Feminist education and the tragedy of Montreal**
◆ **The corporate agenda in Canada's schools**
◆ **Labelling the under-fives**
◆ **Building a socialist curriculum**
◆ **Workers and the rise of mass schooling**
◆ **The teacher-aides' struggle in New Brunswick**
◆ **Growing up male in Nova Scotia**
◆ **Tory cut-backs in Alberta**
◆ **Teacher "grievances" in British Columbia**
◆ **Children's work**
◆ **The politics of standard English in the high school**
◆ **Have the new-left academics sold out?**
◆ **"Going to the dogs" in a northern Ontario school**

In the First Three Years of
OUR SCHOOLS / OUR SELVES
You Will Have Received the Following Books:

✪ *Educating Citizens: A Democratic Socialist Agenda for Canadian Education* by Ken Osbourne

✪ *Building a People's Curriculum: The Experience of a Quebec Teachers' Collective,* by La maîtresse d'école, edited with an introduction by David Clandfield.

✪ *Claiming an Education: Feminism and Canadian Schools,* by Jane Gaskell, Arlene McLaren, Myra Novogrodsky.

✪ *It's Our Own Knowledge: Labour, Public Education & Skills Training,* by Julie Davis, et.al.

✪ *Heritage Languages: The Development and Denial of Canada's Linguistic Resources,* by Jim Cummins and Marcel Danesi.

✪ *What Our High Schools Could Be: A Teacher's Reflections from the 60's to the 90's,* by Bob Davis.

✪ *Their Rightful Place: An Essay on Children and Childcare,* by Loren Lind.

✪ *Techniques of Cooperative Learning,* by Célestin Freinet, edited with an introduction by David Clandfield.

✪ *Taking Charge of the Curriculum: The Challenge for Teachers in B.C.'s School Wars,* by Larry Kuehn.

✪ *A Strategy for Native Education in Canada,* edited by Celia Haig-Brown and Robert Regnier.

✪ *NDP Education Policy: Past, Present and Future,* by William Bruneau and David Clandfield.

✪ *Kids, Sports and the Body,* by Bruce Kidd.

The subscription price for each of these books will be as much as 50% off the bookstore price.

SUBSCRIBE TODAY
GIVE A SUBSCRIPTION FORM TO A FRIEND